Breed Lover's Guide™

BRITTANY

A Practical Guide for the Brittany Lover

Sheila Webster Boneham, Ph.D.

Brittany

Project Team
Editor: Stephanie Fornino
Indexer: Dianne L. Schneider
Book Design: Mary Ann Kahn
Designer: Angela Stanford

TFH Publications®
President/CEO: Glen S. Axelrod
Executive Vice President: Mark E. Johnson
Editor-in-Chief: Albert Connelly, Jr.
Production Manager: Kathy Bontz

TFH Publications, Inc.
One TFH Plaza
Third and Union Avenues
Neptune City, NJ 07753

Printed and bound in China
13 14 15 16   3 5 7 9 8 6 4 2

Library of Congress Cataloging-in-Publication Data
Boneham, Sheila Webster, 1952-
  Brittany / Sheila Webster Boneham.
      p. cm.
  Includes bibliographical references and index.
  ISBN 978-0-7938-4182-0 (alk. paper)
  1. Brittany spaniel. I. Title.
  SF429.B78B66 2011
  636.752--dc22
                          2010013910

This book has been published with the intent to provide accurate and authoritative information in regard to the subject matter within. While every reasonable precaution has been taken in preparation of this book, the author and publisher expressly disclaim responsibility for any errors, omissions, or adverse effects arising from the use or application of the information contained herein. The techniques and suggestions are used at the reader's discretion and are not to be considered a substitute for veterinary care. If you suspect a medical problem consult your veterinarian.

Note: In the interest of concise writing, "he" is used when referring to puppies and dogs unless the text is specifically referring to females or males. "She" is used when referring to people. However, the information contained herein is equally applicable to both sexes.

The Leader In Responsible Animal Care For Over 50 Years!®
www.tfh.com

Table of Contents

Chapter
1

History of
the Brittany

To understand some of the physical and behavioral traits of your Brittany companion, it may be helpful to know a bit about his historical roots. Like the ancestors of other modern breeds, the Brittany's early ancestors were not just companions for their human owners but also vital working partners. The traits that endeared those early dogs to their owners and enabled them to do their assigned tasks effectively are still found in their present-day descendants. Knowing something about his ancestral background will help you to better understand and interact with your Brittany, appreciate his centuries-long heritage, and help him use the characteristics he has inherited to be a well-adjusted and happy member of your family.

The Brittany was named after the anglicized version of the name of the French province (Bretagne) in which his ancestors lived. Although the earliest days of the breed's development are lost in the mists of time, some historians speculate that the human hunters of Brittany may

The Brittany was named after the French province in which his ancestors lived.

WHAT IS A BREED CLUB?

A breed club is an organization of people that works to protect and promote the breed. The national breed club for the Brittany in the United States is the American Brittany Club (ABC), which is a member club of the American Kennel Club (AKC) and the recognized breed sponsor for the American Field's Field Dog Stud Book (FDSB). For more information about the ABC, see http://clubs.akc.org/brit/.

have been using early forebears of today's spaniel and pointing breeds as early as A.D. 150. It is likely that these hunters chose and bred their dogs based on their usefulness for finding game as well as other traits that made them good companions.

Not until the 1600s, though, does clear evidence appear of dogs who closely resemble the modern Brittany. According to some versions of the breed's history, the first naturally bob-tailed ancestor of modern Brittanys was born in the province of Brittany in the mid-19th century, but there is also evidence of small liver-and-white short-tailed spaniels being used in the region much earlier than that. In particular, many paintings and tapestries of the era feature small spaniel-like orange-and-white hunting dogs. In 1850, a Reverend Davies wrote about hunting in Brittany with small moderately coated retrievers that pointed and retrieved game.

The British Invasion

In the late 19th and early 20th centuries, it was a common and accepted practice to cross breeds of dogs with various traits and abilities to create individual, and potentially new, breeds that excelled at particular jobs in specific environments. In fact, such purposeful crosses and subsequent selection of offspring with the sought-after traits are the foundation of nearly all modern breeds.

With the development of better firearms and better modes of transportation in the late 19th and early 20th centuries, it became fashionable for British sportsmen to hunt game birds in France. Naturally, they took their dogs, typically setters and springer spaniels, with them. In 1901, in an effort to prevent the importation of rabies into Britain, a six-month quarantine was enacted on all dogs entering the United Kingdom, making it impossible for the British sportsmen to take their dogs back and forth each year. As a result, the dogs were typically left in the care of French caretakers during the off season. Those dogs were crossed, both accidentally and intentionally, with the smaller native spaniels in an effort to combine the best traits of both.

The offspring tended to be small enough to handle easily, and many were natural pointers and retrievers who trained easily. They retained the eager-to-please attitude of their French forebears, and the strong hunting instincts of the bigger British dogs. Some reports contend that the cross-bred dogs were particularly popular

A BRITTANY BY ANY OTHER NAME

Today there are two distinctly different Brittanys, the French Brittany (Epagneul Breton) and the American Brittany (Brittany). The most obvious difference in the breeds to a casual observer is color: The French Brittany breed standard allows for black pigmentation on the nose and eye rims (even on an orange-and-white dog) and black coloration in the coat, while the American Kennel Club (AKC) standard for the Brittany allows only for orange-and-white or liver-and-white, with pink or brown, never black, pigmentation on the lips, eyelids, and pads of the feet.

The two breeds also vary in size and physical structure. Although their breed standards call for similar size ranges, American Brittanys tend to be a bit taller and heavier than French Brittanys. The American Brittany has a longer muzzle and nose than the French and a bit less slope in the forehead, making the expressions of the two breeds a bit different. The bodies of American Brittanys tend to be a bit longer in proportion to their height than are the bodies of French Brittanys. The latter are characteristically "cobby," or square, with a shorter back that makes for a more compact, muscular look.

The Brittany (American Brittany) is recognized by the AKC, Field Dog Stud Book (FDSB), United Kennel Club (UKC), Canadian Kennel Club (CKC), and a few other registries. The Epagneul Breton (French Brittany) is recognized by the Fédération Cynologique Internationale (FCI), the United Kennel Club (UKC), and many other registries around the world. For more information about the Epagneul Breton, visit the Club Epagneul Breton North America website at www.ceb-usa.org or the French Brittany Gun Dog Association of the United States website at www.frenchbrittany4u.org.

among French peasants who used them to poach game from large estates. However they may have been utilized, these dogs turned out to be well suited for hunters on foot seeking game in open and brushy terrain.

The First Registered Brittany

As the various crosses and their offspring coalesced into a recognizable type of dog, they were registered in France as "miscellaneous French Spaniels." In 1896, a dog named Pincon Royale was exhibited at the Paris Exposition, becoming the first dog to represent the Epagneul Breton (Brittany Spaniel) breed formally. Two years later, Myrrha d'Amorique became the first Epagneul Breton to win first place at a French field trial. The breed was by that time capturing the fancy of a number of French sportsmen, and in 1907 Arthur Enaud and other fanciers of the breed banded together to form the first breed association. Their purpose was to develop a breed standard and to nurture development of the breed and promote it as a distinct breed. In that same year, an orange-and-white dog called "Boy" was registered in France as the first Epagneul Breton.

The 1907 breed standard as first drafted allowed for black in the coat and required dogs to be natural bob-tails. The allowance for black coloration was rejected, however, when the Societé Centrale Canine (French Kennel Club) approved the first official standard for the breed in 1908. Over the next four decades, the breed standard was modified several times to allow for docked tails and other minor adjustments. Then in 1956, in response to persistent pressure from the breed club under the leadership of Gaston Pouchain, the standard for the Epagneul Breton was modified once again to allow black in the coat. Their reasoning was that the breed had black individuals with dark pigment from the earliest days, and there was no good reason to eliminate black

The Brittany arrived in North America after World War I, imported by American sportsmen who had seen the dogs work in their native country.

TIMELINE

- A. D.150: Evidence of hunters using dogs in Brittany.
- 1600s: French artwork shows dogs similar to the Brittany.
- 1850: Reverend Davies writes about hunting with small retrievers in Brittany.
- 1907: First association founded to standardize and promote the Brittany Spaniel in France.
- 1907: "Boy" becomes the first Brittany Spaniel registered with the kennel club in France.
- 1931: The Brittany Spaniel is introduced to the United States.
- 1934–1982: The AKC registers the "Spaniel, Brittany."
- 1982: The American Kennel Club (AKC) drops "Spaniel" from the breed's name.
- 2002: The United Kennel Club (UKC) separates the Brittany and the Epagneul Breton, registering them as two separate breeds.
- 2008: The Brittany ranks 30th out of 156 breeds on the AKC's registration list.

dogs from the breeding pool. Under the current standards for the Epagneul Breton as recognized by various kennel clubs outside the United States, and since 2002 by the United Kennel Club (UKC) in this country, black remains acceptable in the coat and skin pigment.

The Brittany in America

The Brittany arrived in North America after World War I, imported by American sportsmen who had seen the dogs work in their native country. The different hunting conditions in the United States created a preference among hunters for a different style of hunting dog and, by extension, field trial dog. American hunters and breeders preferred a larger, longer-bodied dog than the French, perhaps because of the different terrain and, to some extent, their longer experience with the larger setters and pointers used in North America for hunting game birds. By selecting for greater size and body length and certain other conformation differences, over several generations American breeders created a breed that is now considered completely separate and different in important ways from the Epagneul Breton, or French Brittany.

In 1934, the American Kennel Club (AKC) recognized the breed, classifying it as a sporting dog, and using the name "Spaniel, Brittany." Many fanciers argued that because spaniels are flushing dogs and Brittanys point and retrieve but do not flush birds, the name was a misnomer. In 1982, at the request of the American Brittany Club, "Spaniel" was dropped and the official name of the American breed became "Brittany."

The American Brittany breed standard, like the old French standard, allows only orange-and-white or liver-and-white coat coloration and pink to tan pigmentation of the skin. Because hunting conditions tend to be different in the United States than in Europe and because pointing-breed field trials in the United States tend to be conducted from horseback, the Brittany standard also calls for a slightly bigger, leggier dog with certain other modifications in structure. By the 1970s, the Brittany in the United States had become essentially a new breed, closely related to but clearly different from the French Brittany (See sidebar "A Brittany by Any Other Name.") Despite changes in the breed, though, the Brittany remains a versatile and highly accomplished show dog and hunting dog, a loyal and gentle household companion, and a terrific teammate for a wide variety of canine sports and activities.

Ask the Expert

WHAT'S IN A NAME?

Kennel clubs around the world have different opinions about what should be in a breed's name. The dog we know in the United States as the Brittany goes by different names in different places and even different times. In the United States, the Brittany was known as the Brittany Spaniel (officially, "Spaniel, Brittany") from 1934 to 1982, and many people still use the old name. While the American Kennel Club (AKC) recognizes only the Brittany, the United Kennel Club (UKC) in 2002 separated the Brittany and the Epagneul Breton into separate recognized breeds with different breed standards. In Canada, the breed we call the Brittany is still known as the Brittany Spaniel or, more officially, as the Spaniel (Brittany). The kennel clubs of Britain and Australia use the name Brittany. Many countries' kennel clubs do not recognize the American Brittany but follow the Fédération Cynologique Internationale (World Canine Organization) in recognizing the Epagneul Breton (French Brittany).

Chapter
2

Characteristics of the Brittany

E very dog is an individual, and the Brittany in your life is no exception. But dogs of any breed also share a range of physical and behavioral traits with other members of their extended family. Those breed traits help define the breed. They also place the breed within a larger group of breeds—Brittanys share many characteristics with other sporting or gundogs used for hunting game birds and other small game. But the specific set of traits common to a breed also serves to distinguish members of the breed from dogs of any other breed or mixture of breeds. In fact, that's what makes a breed: highly predictable characteristics that are passed from generation to generation.

Physical Characteristics

Listed in this section are the traits that make a Brittany a Brittany.

Size

One trait that attracts many people to the Brittany is his moderate size. Ideally, the Brittany stands between 17.5 and 20.5 inches (44.5 and 52 cm) tall at the withers, which is the high point behind the base of the neck where the shoulder blades meet. The physically fit Brittany weighs in at 30 to 40 pounds (13.5 to 18 kg) and has moderate bone structure, neither delicate nor heavy.

Body Structure

The Brittany's body is compact, and he is rather long-legged in proportion to his length, and his back slopes slightly downward toward the rear. In fact, if you measure your Brittany, his height at the withers should equal his length from sternum (breastbone) to backside. These proportions enable the Brittany to cover a lot of ground with his long stride and make him very agile. Some Brittanys are born with little or no tail; others traditionally have their tails docked to about 4 inches (10 cm).

One trait that attracts many people to the Brittany is his moderate size.

REHOMED BRITTANYS

Q: What is one of the most common reasons that people decide to rehome their pet Brittanys?

A: "A lot of people give up their Brittanys because the dogs have so much energy," says Shannon Ridener, a volunteer with National Brittany Rescue and Adoption Network (NBRAN). "Some people don't research the breed before they get a Brittany and don't realize that these are highly active dogs." Ridener stresses the need for people to "do their research before adopting a Brittany or any other dog. Make sure it's a good fit for your family's lifestyle before you decide to bring one home." If you already have a Brittany, be sure that he gets plenty of daily exercise—you'll both be happier.

Coat

The Brittany's coat is moderate in length, dense, and straight or wavy but not curly. It should be medium in texture, neither too silky soft nor too wiry. It should be long enough to protect his skin from burs and thorns but not so long that it becomes a liability in heavy brush. Although the backs of the legs are feathered, the feathering is not heavy compared to that of many other breeds, and is usually kept trimmed to a reasonable length for easier grooming. (See Chapter 5.)

Coat Color

American Brittanys registered with the American Kennel Club (AKC) may be orange (a light red) and white or liver (dark red-brown) and white, and the colored areas may have roaning (white hairs mixed in with the color). Some ticking—spots or freckles—is considered desirable by fans of the breed. Occasionally a liver Brittany has orange markings on the eyebrows, muzzle, and cheeks; this is known as "tricolor" because three colors—liver, white, and orange—are present. Although black is allowed in French Brittanys (see Chapter 1), it is a disqualification in the AKC show ring.

Head

The Brittany's head should also be moderate. The skull is medium in length and slightly narrower than it is long. A broad, coarse head is undesirable, as is a narrow head. Like all other bird dogs, the Brittany should have a soft expression, alert and eager but never

Like most other bird-hunting breeds, Brittanys are generally happy, alert, upbeat dogs.

hard, aggressive, or suspicious. The eyes themselves should never bulge or appear pop-eyed, as that would expose them more to injury from dense brush when hunting. They should be protected by fairly heavy, highly expressive eyebrows. For the same reason, the eyelids should be tight, never droopy. Dark eyes are considered preferable, but lighter brown or amber eyes are allowed unless they are so pale that they ruin the dog's soft expression. The short, triangular, slightly rounded ears should lie flat and should be set high on the skull, above the level of the eyes. When pulled forward, the ears should reach about half the length of the muzzle. They should be densely covered with short hair and have very little fringe, or feathering.

Living With Your Brittany

Every dog is, naturally, more than his physical looks. In fact, personality and behavior are far more important to happy canine/human relations. Experienced Brittany owners, rescuers, and breeders emphasize that the Brittany is a marvelous dog, but he's not the right dog for everyone.

Remember, though, that any description of personality and behavior in a family—whether a breed of dog or your very own human family—is really just a general average. Each individual is different. If you survey experienced owners, breeders, and rescuers of Brittanys, you'll find that it's hard to generalize. That's why if you are looking for a new Brittany it will be to your advantage, and that of your future dog, to go to a knowledgeable breeder or rescuer who can help you choose the right individual puppy or dog for you and your lifestyle.

Now, with that caveat in mind, let's take a look at the traits that transcend the breed's beauty and make him a certain kind of companion.

Brittany Personality

Like most other bird-hunting breeds, Brittanys are generally happy, alert, upbeat dogs. Although your Brittany may not be everyone's instant best friend, he should be friendly to people and other animals, and neither aggressive nor shy.

Some individual Brittanys are extremely energetic, especially when young, and such dogs need lots of physical and mental stimulation. Others are more mellow, although don't expect a young Brittany to be a couch potato. Given enough exercise, though, even active Brittanys generally make excellent house dogs and will settle down when they come inside with their families. Many Brittanys hunt and perform in field competitions, then come home to live as house pets the rest of the time.

In fact, your Brittany needs to be with his family. These are dogs who bond closely with people, and they need attention every day, not just to their physical needs but to their emotional needs as well. If you fail to give your dog his share of attention, you may end up having to deal with behavior problems such as barking, digging, destructive chewing, and a whole host of others. Besides, why bring such a loving companion into your life and then deprive him of your company?

People often wonder which makes a better pet, a male or female Brittany. Some people do have strong preferences for one sex or the other, but breeders, rescuers, and owners of Brittanys generally agree that the individual dog is far more important than its sex, especially once the dog is spayed or neutered. Both males and females are loyal, loving, and affectionate, and both make wonderful companions wherever you take them.

Companionability

Most well-socialized Brittanys like people, and most are playful but gentle with children. Both dogs and children must, of course, be taught to play kindly and safely with one another, and all interaction

PUPPY OR ADULT?

Many people automatically think "puppy" when the time comes to find a new canine companion. Baby Brittanys are adorable, that's for sure. They are also a lot of work. If you have the time, energy, and patience to devote to the needs of a young dog, a puppy may be the right choice. If you've never raised a dog from puppyhood through adolescence, or if it's been a long time since you did, you need to know that a puppy is a big responsibility. For many people, an adult Brittany is a better option.

A young puppy is a lot like a human infant. He will need trips outside in the wee hours of the morning for housetraining. He will probably have a few accidents in the house—he's a baby, after all, and doesn't have complete control. He may

cry for the first few nights in your home because he was used to sleeping with his mom and siblings. As he travels through adolescence, a Brittany pup needs plenty of exercise every single day. He will need careful supervision as he learns what he may and may not do as a member of your household. He will need training to understand what you want from him, and he will need to be socialized carefully during his first two years and especially during the critical period from his 8th to 16th weeks. (See Chapter 6.)

People also tend to want puppies because, people think, puppies can be shaped through their upbringing. Socialization, training, and other aspects of good care do help a puppy reach his potential, but unless you're very experienced, it's hard to predict exactly what an individual puppy's potential really is. We can shape the adult dog's personality to only a limited degree, because his genetic makeup, which is determined at conception, affects not only his looks but also his temperament, personality, intelligence, and behavior. You can improve the odds that your dog will mature as you hope by working with an ethical, knowledgeable breeder and raising your pup well, but predicting adult traits is not an exact science.

When you choose an adult Brittany from a rescue organization, shelter, or breeder,

what you see is pretty much what you get. Although many dogs who come through rescue become more confident and improve physically with better food, care, and training, the dog's essential traits are usually already apparent. Brittanys tend to adapt well to new situations, and most adult dogs bond to their new families with little trouble. If you don't have the time or inclination to spend two years giving a puppy the best possible start in life, consider adopting an adult. Better yet, consider a senior rescued dog, who will likely be a bit more settled than his younger brethren and still full of love. Some terrific older puppies and adults are available from Brittany rescue organizations, and breeders will sometimes offer retired show dogs to pet homes for a nominal fee after having them altered.

between your dog and children, especially young children or those you don't know well, should be closely supervised for the safety of both.

Brittanys also typically enjoy the companionship of other dogs. Again, proper socialization is important. (See Chapter 6.) Individual dogs, like individual people, may respond differently to other individuals, so be cautious when introducing your Brittany to new dogs. Be aware, too, that your Brittany's natural hunting instinct may cause him to see active small dogs as potential prey until he gets to know them, so always maintain control of your dog around small dogs until you are confident that he won't "hunt" them. The same goes for cats; always introduce your Brittany carefully to new cats, keep control, and make sure that the cat has an escape route. The same cautions apply if you have smaller pets, such as rabbits or birds, in your home.

Environment

People often ask whether a Brittany will live happily in a particular environment, such as an apartment, a big suburban back yard, or a farm. The answer is that the best place for a Brittany is with a person or family who will give him what he needs to live a full, healthy life: good food, health care, exercise, grooming,

training, and, most of all, love and affection.

The physical environment can, naturally, make a difference to an individual owner's ability to provide for a Brittany's needs. Most young Brittanys have lots of energy, and they need safe ways to use that energy on a daily basis. As a Brittany owner, you must see that your dog gets the exercise he needs. If you have a fenced yard, a couple of

Brittanys need plenty of exercise as well as mental stimulation.

games a day of fetch the tennis ball may do the trick. If you don't have a yard where you can safely play running games with your dog, you'll have to find other ways to exercise him. Even if you do have a safely fenced yard, you can't just send your dog out the door and tell him to run around. Most dogs either stand and stare at the door or engage in undesirable behaviors, such as recreational barking or creative landscaping. Your Brittany wants a playmate, and unless you have other dogs who will romp around the yard with him, you need to go out and play with your dog. But that's half the fun, isn't it?

Your Brittany will thrive as your household companion. Dogs are social animals, and your dog needs the companionship of his family, human and otherwise. Banishing a dog to a back yard, basement, or other isolated place not only is cruel but also often leads to a variety of unwanted behaviors, including destructive digging or chewing and neurotic behaviors like pacing and nonstop barking. Make your Brittany your true companion and he'll more than repay you with love, loyalty, and better behavior.

Exercise Requirements

The Brittany was developed to be capable of following his excellent nose through fields and brush to find and indicate game birds to hunters with guns. He has plenty of energy and stamina and a desire to do his hereditary job. For the pet owner, that translates to a dog who needs lots of exercise as well as opportunities to put his mind to work.

Brittanys do vary in their exercise needs, and they don't all need to run flat out for hours every day. In their first few years, though, most Brittanys do need 20 to 30 minutes of running exercise two or three times a day. As your Brittany ages, he may be happy with less exercise, although some individuals remain very active well into adulthood. Your Brittany is likely to live 12 to 14 years and will require some exercise and lots of attention throughout that time.

There are, of course, many ways to provide exercise for your dog. Just remember that you need to be part of the program—most dogs do not self-exercise when shoved out into the back yard alone, and those who do often engage in undesirable activities like barking, digging, escaping the yard to run loose, and so on. Happily, half the fun of having a Brittany is playing with him. (See Chapter 8 for ideas that will take you beyond neighborhood walks and games of fetch.)

Keep rescued Brittanys in mind too if you want a Brittany but aren't sure you want the energy of a puppy or adolescent. Many wonderful adult dogs are in rescue through no fault of their own, and one of

FAST FACTS

- ✓ The Brittany is a physically moderate dog in all ways.
- ✓ Brittanys are generally happy, alert companions.
- ✓ Brittanys tend to be high-energy dogs who need a fair amount of exercise.
- ✓ Brittanys thrive when kept close as companions to their people.
- ✓ Brittanys typically are easy to train and willing to please.
- ✓ The Brittany is a true dual-purpose dog.

them might be your perfect dog. Each dog in a bonafide Brittany rescue program is evaluated while in his foster home to help make the best possible matches between dogs and adopters. For more information, visit American Brittany Rescue at www.americanbrittanyrescue.org.

Trainability

Brittanys are known and highly valued by their fans for their biddability, or willingness to please their people. Still, they aren't born knowing what people want them to do. That's where you come in—it's your job to teach your Brittany what he needs to know to make you happy.

Obedience training is recommended for all Brittanys, regardless of the role your dog will play in your life. (See Chapter 6.) Basic obedience training not only will teach your dog what you want him to do but also will teach you a lot about your dog and strengthen the bond between

the two of you. Nor is training just for pups—older dogs are avid learners and often better able to focus on the lessons at hand. As long as your dog is mobile and aware, it's never too late to begin training or to teach new things.

Brittanys respond with great enthusiasm to positive methods of training that reward success rather than punishing mistakes (see Chapter 6), so look for a class or trainer who uses positive motivational methods. Keep in mind, too, that the more you teach your dog, whether parlor tricks or advanced competition skills, the easier it will be for him to learn the next new task. Make learning fun for your dog and you'll find that it's fun for you as well.

What Your Brittany Is Bred For

The Brittany is, above all else, an excellent hunting dog, and he has many admirers because of his skill in the field. Experienced hunters say that the Brittany is a good breed for a neophyte hunter because he is highly biddable and he instinctively knows the main part of his responsibility in the field, which is to point and hold game for the hunter and to retrieve game on land and in the water. He is smaller and has a shorter range and less stamina than the bigger pointing breeds, but those traits, along with his excellent nose for finding birds, suit him well to modern hunting conditions that often involve less open land. Although not every individual dog is a great hunter, with adequate training most Brittanys have enough natural ability to become at least average hunting dogs.

Unlike some breeds that have a sharp division between "working" and "show" lines, Brittanys tend to be "dual-quality" dogs. Many of the champions you see in the conformation ring also hunt or compete in field trials, and many of the top hunting and field trial Brittanys can hold their own in the show ring. Indeed, more Brittanys have achieved the lofty AKC title of Dual Champion (meaning the dog has earned championships in both the conformation ring and in field trials)

than all other Sporting Group breeds combined.

For owners who are not interested in hunting, the Brittany's intelligent, biddable nature makes him a wonderful candidate not only as a pet but also for such sports as obedience, rally, tracking, agility, and, for the younger set, junior showmanship or 4H. For those with a less competitive bent, the breed's typically gentle, friendly demeanor also makes the well-socialized Brittany a wonderful candidate for dog-assisted therapy work.

If you don't yet have your Brittany and you are interested in participating in one or more sporting or other activities with your dog, be sure to discuss your plans with your breeder or rescue representative to obtain help in choosing the right puppy or dog. If you already have a Brittany, go ahead and give some activities a try. Even if you have no interest in competing, going to classes and training your dog beyond basic obedience will be lots of fun for both of you. Learning new things together will enhance the bond between you and your Brittany and add a new dimension to your appreciation for this wonderful breed.

Chapter 3

Supplies for Your Brittany

Whether your new Brittany is a puppy or an adult, stocking up on supplies before you bring him home will make the transition go more smoothly for the whole family, leaving you plenty of time to play and bond with your new family member and begin his training. Let's take a look at some of the stuff your dog will need.

Baby Gates

Until your Brittany is fully reliable in the house, you'll want to make sure that he stays wherever you are. Even when he's fully trained, there may be areas of your home where you'd rather he didn't go. You can shut doors, of course, but a baby gate or two are very useful for keeping your Brittany in certain parts of the house and out of others. If you have a cat, a baby gate makes it easy to provide a dog-free zone for kitty's food, litter box, and naps.

Baby gates are available from most discount, hardware, and baby supply stores and come in wood and plastic. Many pet-supply stores and catalogs also offer gates, including specially designed gates for wider door openings, permanent mounting on the doorframe, and other special situations.

Bed

Dog beds come in a wide variety of styles, from thin pads to orthopedic foam to soft, loosely padded pillows. Prices also range widely. Of course, your dog's favorite place to sleep won't be based on price or a fancy label but on how it suits his own idea of comfort. That being the case, don't spend a lot on a doggy bed until you have a good idea of where your Brittany likes to lie down in your home. Does he like the unpadded coolness of the bare kitchen floor? Or does he like to sink into the soft cushions on your sofa? There's no point spending money on a bed your dog won't use.

When you do zero in on the right kind of bed, be sure that it is large enough to let your Brittany stretch out and relax. Be sure, too, that the whole bed is washable or that it has a removable washable cover. Keeping your dog's bed clean will help with flea and tick control (see Chapter 5) and will help prevent "doggy odor" in your house.

If you have a puppy or young dog who likes to chew and rip things up, wait until he outgrows this phase before you buy him a bed. He'll sleep fine on the floor or the bottom of his crate.

Collars and Harnesses

Your Brittany needs at least one collar. The safest basic collar for everyday wear is a "flat collar" made of nylon, fabric, or leather and fastened with a buckle or a quick-release fastener. This is the

A flat collar that fastens with a buckle is a good choice for your Brittany.

collar that your dog should wear with identification and license tags attached. If you train using positive methods and rewards (please do!), you will probably want to use a second flat collar without tags for training.

Check the collar's fit frequently, especially while your dog is growing, and readjust or replace it when it no longer fits. You should be able to insert two fingers between the collar and your dog's neck. Tighter than that is too tight for comfort and safety, and a collar that hangs looser than that can get caught on things and trap or strangle your dog.

Other types of collars are readily available in pet supply and other stores, including training collars (also called "choke chains" or "slip" chains or collars), pinch or prong collars, and even electronic "shock" collars. Used incorrectly, they can easily injure or frighten your dog, causing behavior problems and setting his training back. You and your Brittany will both be happier if you spend your money on a good obedience class rather than collars that hurt your dog to make him behave.

Many people now use halter-style devices to control their dogs and keep

TRAINING TREATS

Q: I need to buy some training treats to reward my Brittany in training sessions. What should I use?

A: "The short answer is 'anything your dog likes!'" says professional dog trainer Clarice Kashuba. "I recommend small, low-calorie treats. Larger treats work well, too, as long as they can be broken into small pieces. Some dogs like little pieces of apple or carrot. Keep in mind that treats should make up no more than 10 percent of your dog's daily diet. You can avoid empty calories by using regular dog food, perhaps in a different flavor such as fish and sweet potato, fed from your hand as a treat. Rolled dog food is also a good treat; it is nutritionally balanced, can be cut into small pieces, and has a taste that most dogs love. When you are teaching something new or difficult or want to reward a particularly good behavior (like coming when called in the middle of a squirrel chase), use a 'high-value' treat—something extra wonderful, like a bit of hot dog or cheese." Kashuba, who owns Flying Colors Dog Training in Indiana, also notes that "toys and play are also rewarding for your dog—anything that makes him happy can be used as a reward."

them from pulling. Although a properly fitted head halter can work well in some cases, I see far too many dogs struggling against halters that do not fit them properly, resulting in pinching and pulling of facial skin. In addition, there is some evidence that improperly used head halters can cause serious cervical, middle ear, and brain stem injuries. And all too often the control afforded in most cases by a head halter takes the place of real training, so if the halter isn't on (or comes off!), all control is lost. I highly recommend, again, good obedience training instead.

A harness may be useful while your Brittany is very young but really gives you control only as long as you are able to restrain him from pulling. A harness is not a training device, and in an adolescent or adult dog, it's not very useful for control either.

Crates

A crate (sometimes called a carrier, kennel, or cage) is a vital piece of equipment for the responsible dog owner. A crate will be particularly useful while your Brittany is a puppy and adolescent, but adult dogs, too, need their crates at times. Used properly, a crate simplifies housetraining. It also provides a safe and familiar place to confine your dog if he's ill or injured, or in other circumstances. A crate in your vehicle will keep your Brittany comfortable while traveling and safer in an accident than he would be loose in the car.

Dog crates come in wire, plastic, and aluminum, on wheels, with handles, and in various colors and sizes. Your dog should have room to stand up, lie down, and turn around comfortably in his crate, but he doesn't need much more than that. For an adult Brittany, that would mean a crate approximately 22 inches (56 cm) wide by 32 inches (81 cm) long by 23 inches (58.5 cm) high (sometimes known as a #300 crate). For a young puppy who is being housetrained, you may want a smaller crate, or you can block off part of his adult-sized crate to limit his space and encourage cleanliness. For more about crate training, see Chapter 6.

To keep your dog safe and secure, check that the door fits well and

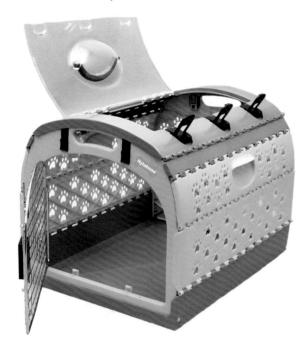

Plastic crates may be helpful for housetraining a puppy.

RESTRAINING YOUR PUPPY

Never use a choke chain, prong collar, or head halter on a young puppy—you can cause permanent injuries to his delicate throat and spine. Use a flat collar, and use it gently.

latches securely. Most people like to provide bedding in the crate, but during housetraining it's often better not to provide absorbent bedding. Similarly, if your Brittany likes to rip up his bedding, leave it out. Some dogs even prefer the bare floor of the crate. Small washable nonslip rugs make great crate bedding.

Dishes

Dishes for serving your dog water and food come in many forms, and as with dog beds, prices range from free (something you already have and "repurpose" for your pup) to very expensive designer dishes. Here is a summary of good and not-so-great traits of the types of dishes commonly available.

- Stainless steel dishes are sturdy, chew proof, easy to clean, and dishwasher safe, and they last practically forever—my first choice by far.
- Plastic dishes are lightweight and cheap. Unfortunately, many dogs like to chew them. They can also be difficult to clean thoroughly, and bacteria can build up in cracks and scratches in the plastic. Finally, some

plastic dishes release chemicals into the food and water they contain, and some dogs are allergic to plastic.

- Ceramic dishes are pretty, but they are also breakable, and some ceramics made outside the United States contain lead and other toxins that can leach into food and water. I would not recommend ceramic.

Don't worry about purchasing small puppy dishes—your Brittany puppy can manage fine with an adult-sized dish.

Stainless steel dishes are sturdy, chewproof, easy to clean, and dishwasher safe.

If you want to restrict your puppy's movement try an ex-pen.

Exercise Pen

If you want to restrict your puppy or older dog's movement but want to give him a bit more room than a crate offers, consider an exercise pen, or "ex-pen," which is an enclosure made of linked sections. When not in use, an ex-pen can be folded for storage or transport.

Traditional ex-pens are made of wire panels, but ex-pens are also available in lighter-weight plastics and fabric. They come in different heights; for a young puppy, 24 inches (61 cm) usually works. For an adult dog, 36 to 48 inches (91.5 to 122 cm) is more secure.

If you do use an ex-pen, be aware that many dogs learn to climb or jump out of them or to lift them and crawl underneath. Tops are available to prevent escapes by climbing, and you can sometimes anchor an ex-pen to the ground. Still, an ex-pen is not as secure as a built fence, so *never* trust it to confine your Brittany when you aren't nearby, especially outdoors.

Food and Food-Storage Containers

You'll need high-quality commercial food or ingredients for a high-quality homemade diet based on advice from your dog's breeder, your veterinarian, and books and Internet sources written by qualified canine nutritionists. Food should be stored away from heat to prevent deterioration and should be kept secure from vermin.

Grooming Supplies

You'll need at least one brush, a comb, nail clippers, a mild shampoo formulated for dogs, and doggy toothbrush and toothpaste.

Identification

No matter how careful you are, your Brittany could get away sometime. And because Brittanys, like other pointing breeds, are built to run, your dog could travel a considerable distance once he's on the loose. If that happens, you'll

want whoever finds your dog to know that you are looking for him, so make it as easy as you can for someone to contact you. Although we now have many high-tech options for canine identification, the simplest thing is still an old-fashioned identification tag on your dog's collar. Have it engraved with your name, address, and telephone number(s). You might also want to include your dog's name and your e-mail address. You should also attach your dog's current rabies tag, and if required where you live, his license tag to his collar. Some people also attach medical alert tags for dogs with special health-care needs, such as diabetes. Many pet supply companies also offer collars custom embroidered with your dog's name and phone number. That would eliminate the need for an ID tag, but you should still attach your dog's rabies and license tags. One of the latest ID gadgets is a high-speed digital device that can be removed from your dog's collar and plugged into the USB port on any computer. All of these collar-borne IDs work.

The downside of collars and tags is that they can be lost or removed, so many pet owners choose a form of permanent identification as backup. Despite the increased numbers of dog owners sporting tats, tattoos are not as commonly used as they used to be

Have your dog's ID engraved with your name, address, and telephone number(s).

SUPPLIES CHECKLIST

If you're like most other dog owners, you will buy lots of other stuff for your Brittany as time goes by, but to get started you'll need the following supplies:

- ✓ a dog bed or two for your home
- ✓ a license to attach to his collar if required where you live
- ✓ an identification tag to fasten to his collar
- ✓ at least one collar, possibly two (one for everyday wear and another for training)
- ✓ at least one crate (possibly two or more, but especially one for home and one for the car)
- ✓ at least one leash; a spare is a good idea

- ✓ bedding for inside the crate(s)
- ✓ grooming supplies: brush, comb, nail clippers, mild dog shampoo, doggy toothbrush and toothpaste
- ✓ high-quality food and treats
- ✓ possibly an exercise pen
- ✓ possibly at least one baby gate
- ✓ safe toys and chewies
- ✓ safe, nonbreakable dishes for food and water

to identify dogs. This is partly because simpler options have become easily available, and partly because even if someone sees the tattoo, they have to know whom to call to find out who registered the tattoo number. Still, a tattoo on a dog's belly or inner flank (the most commonly used locations) is an effective proof of ownership. For more information about tattoo registries, contact Tattoo-A-Pet at 800-828-8667 or visit its website at www.tattoo-a-pet.com.

Much more common today is the microchip, a transmitter about the

size of a grain of rice that is inserted by syringe under the skin over the shoulders. Each microchip is encoded with a unique number that you register to your dog. The chip can be read by a special scanner, which most shelters and many veterinarians have. The two most commonly used microchip ID programs are:

- PETtrac/AVID Microchips, 800-336-2843, http://www.avidid.com/pets/index.html
- HomeAgain MicroChips/Companion Animal Recovery, 800-252-7894, www.public.homeagain.com

For more information, contact the companies or your veterinarian.

Leashes

A good leash is a basic tool for both training and your dog's safety. Using a leash in public places is also a social responsibility, not only because many communities have laws requiring that dogs be leashed but also because not everyone you meet—human, canine, or others—really wants a close encounter with your dog. No matter how reliable you think your Brittany is, *always* leash him when outside walls or a fence. A ten-second squirrel chase into the street could end in tragedy.

You need at least one leash, and it doesn't hurt to have one or two spares. A well-made 4- to 6-foot (1- to 2-m) leather leash 1/4- to 1/2-inch (0.5- to 1.5-cm) wide is strong, relatively gentle on your hands, and useful for most training and walking situations. Nylon leashes are inexpensive, but some are abrasive and can burn or scrape your skin, so check the feel of the leash in your hands before you purchase one. Cotton leashes are also available and are usually a bit easier on the hands than nylon. Retractable leashes are handy for walking where there is room for your dog to range a little wider, but because there is always some tension on the leash when it isn't locked, retractable leashes encourage dogs to pull. If your Brittany tends to pull on the leash, wait until you have trained him to walk nicely on a slack leash before using a retractable. If you do use a retractable leash, check it frequently for damage and replace it when it shows wear to the cords. I've heard of serious injuries caused when a retractable leash broke and snapped back.

Some stores sell chain leashes, but they're ineffective as training tools. They are also heavy and can injure you or your dog. Leave them on the racks.

Toys and Chewies

Finally—the fun stuff! Although puppies and many adult dogs will play with almost anything portable, your Brittany will be safer and you'll no doubt be a lot happier if you give him safe toys and teach him to leave your other possessions alone. All toys, including balls, should be too big for your dog

Your Brittany will be safer and you'll no doubt be a lot happier if you give him safe toys and teach him to leave your other possessions alone.

You need at least one leash for your dog.

to swallow. Check frequently for loose parts—dogs have died or required emergency surgery after swallowing things they shouldn't swallow, including toys and parts of toys. Loose stuffing, ribbons, plastic squeakers, and other plastic parts are especially dangerous. If your puppy or dog is aggressive about ripping toys apart, give him only toys designed for dogs who play roughly, and check them frequently. Don't leave him with anything he could pull apart and swallow when you are gone—stick with tough, well-made chew toys. Replace chew toys when they develop cracks or sharp points or edges or when they become small enough to swallow. Individual dogs like different types of chew toys, so if your Brittany doesn't like one kind of chewie, try another.

Chapter 4

Feeding Your Brittany

Your Brittany may not "be what he eats," but nutrition does play a vital role in his health and behavior from conception through old age. Problems such as dry skin and coat, itchiness, hot spots (sores), loose stools, hyperactivity, and lack of energy affect too many pet dogs and are often the result of poor diet. Healthful food, on the other hand, will help your Brittany remain healthy throughout his life.

Basic Canine Nutrition

You can do two important things to be sure that your Brittany's diet is supporting his health. First, learn the basics of canine nutrition. Then observe how your dog looks and acts; if something doesn't seem right, consider whether the problem could be something in, or not in, his food.

Dogs are carnivores; when they live wild they kill and eat prey animals. But don't let that fool you—your dog needs

Carbohydrates give your Brittany energy.

VITAMINS AND NUTRITIONAL SUPPLEMENTS

Q: Should I give my Brittany vitamins or other nutritional supplements?

A: According to veterinarian Lisa A. Notestine, DVM, MT (ASCP), "Vitamin and mineral supplements are generally not necessary if you are feeding a high-quality commercial dog food. However, a dog's nutritional requirements depend on a number of factors, including age, activity level, pregnancy, and medical conditions. Be sure to consult with your veterinarian to determine the best diet for your Brittany."

more than meat to thrive. A well-balanced canine diet includes carbohydrates, fats, minerals, proteins, vitamins, and water. Let's see what each of these nutrients does for your dog.

Carbohydrates

Carbohydrates provide energy and are found primarily in vegetables, grains, and fruits. Although dogs and other carnivores need the nutrients found in plants, their digestive systems cannot break down the tough cellulose in plant matter. In the wild, they eat partially digested plant matter from the stomachs and intestines of their prey. Domesticated carnivores, including your Brittany, rely on us to cook their vegetables and fruits so that they can utilize the nonmeat nutrients that are essential for good health. Common sources of carbohydrates in commercial dog foods include corn, soy beans, wheat, and

rice. Because some dogs are allergic to one or more of these commonly used grains, foods are also available commercially that use alternative sources of carbohydrates, including potatoes, oats or oatmeal, various other grains, vegetables, and fruits. If you feed your dog a homemade diet, you can, of course, choose from a wide variety of carbohydrate sources.

Fats

Although you don't want your Brittany to become obese, the right amount of dietary fat is critical to good health. Fats provide energy, help transport other nutrients throughout the body, and help cushion the internal organs and insulate them against cold. Meats, milk, butter, and vegetable oils, fed in proper balance with other foods, are good sources of dietary fats.

There are a number of less-well-known foods that offer higher-quality ingredients at a more reasonable cost.

Minerals

Minerals build and maintain strong bones, strengthen cell tissue, and help your dog's internal organs function properly. If your dog eats a high-quality diet, he's unlikely to suffer a mineral deficiency, so don't add vitamin or mineral supplements to his diet unless your veterinarian recommends them. An excess of minerals can cause serious problems, including permanent bone deformities, especially in growing puppies.

Proteins

Proteins are vital building blocks for a healthy, lean body. The best sources of complete proteins, which contain all of the essential amino acids, are meats, fish, poultry, milk, cheese, yogurt, fish meal, and eggs, although plant products also provide some of the amino acids. Your Brittany's diet should be about 18 to 25 percent protein.

Vitamins

Vitamins are chemical compounds essential to good health. Fruits are an excellent source of vitamins, as are the livers of most animals. A high-quality diet will provide the vitamins your Brittany needs, and, as with minerals, vitamin supplements should not be given unless your veterinarian advises you to do so. It is important to store food properly and to use it before its expiration date, though, because light, heat, moisture, and rancidity can destroy vitamins.

Water

We don't usually think of water as a nutrient, but it is critical for life and good health. Your Brittany gets much of his water directly by drinking, but he also uses metabolic water, which is the water released from food as it is digested. Although you may want to limit his water at certain times while housetraining him, in general your dog should have access to cool clean water at all times because he loses water through panting and elimination. He needs to replenish that water to keep his body in balance and his organs functioning properly.

What to Feed Your Brittany

When it comes to canine diets, we and our dogs are fortunate to have many options. Dogs can thrive on commercial foods or homemade, or a combination. Let's see whether we can sniff out the option that will work best for you and your Brittany.

Commercial Dog Foods

Dog food is big business, as a count of expensive television ads and a quick check of the dog food aisle in any pet supply store will verify. Every manufacturer claims to have the single best food for dogs everywhere, yet ingredients and prices vary widely. How to choose?

The truth is that commercial dog foods vary from the canine equivalent of junk food (low-quality ingredients, nutritionally empty fillers, dyes, and other chemicals) to very high-quality formulas (human-grade ingredients free of non-nutritional "junk"). Most, including many of the best-known foods, are somewhere in the middle.

As with any commercial product, high quality costs more than poor, but price isn't the whole story. Remember, just because a beautiful television ad says such and such food is best doesn't make it so! Before you spring for the famous-name dog food, check the labels carefully. There are a number of less-well-known foods that offer higher-quality ingredients at a more reasonable cost.

Keep in mind that cheap foods tend to offer fewer meat proteins, fewer vitamins, more fat, and more fillers. A dog fed such a diet will probably live a shorter life and may suffer from health and behavior problems that are often linked to a poor diet, including cancer,

FEEDING PUPPIES AND ADOLESCENTS

Young puppies simply can't put enough food into their tummies in one or two meals to provide the nutrition they need every day to promote healthy growth and development. Most breeders and vets therefore recommend that puppies 7 to 16 weeks eat three or four meals spaced evenly through the waking hours of the day, with the last meal at least two hours before bedtime to make housetraining easier. Between four and six months of age, your pup needs two or three meals a day, and by the time he's six months old, your puppy should do fine on two meals a day. Monitor your Brittany's growth, weight, and condition closely while he is growing and maturing during his first two years. He should be neither skinny nor fat, his bones and muscles should appear to be strong, his coat should be full and glossy, and he should be active and alert. If not, see your vet as soon as possible.

allergies, hyperactivity, lethargy, and damage to various organs. Higher-quality dog foods use better ingredients and contain few if any fillers, chemicals, or dyes. Because they are easier to digest, your dog will be better able to utilize the nutrients in the food and will also produce smaller, better-formed stools and be less flatulent. Higher-quality foods cost more per bag, or can, than lesser-quality foods, but because better foods are more nutritionally dense, your dog won't need to eat as much per meal. In the long run, too, you will spend less money on veterinary care.

Commercial dog foods come in four common forms.

Dry Dog Foods (Kibble)

Dry dog food, or kibble, is the least expensive form of commercial dog food (compared to the equivalent-quality canned or frozen foods). Dry food should be stored in an airtight container, protected from heat and light, and used by its expiration date, but it does not need to be refrigerated. A high-quality dry food without fillers will result in firmer, smaller stools, making cleanup easier for you and housetraining easier for both you and your dog.

Semi-Moist Foods

Semi-moist dog foods are typically soft chunks packaged in serving-size packets. There's not much good about them except convenience. These foods are comparatively expensive and result in large, soft, smelly stools. The soft food tends to stick to the teeth, often causing gum disease and tooth decay, and they often contain dyes, chemical preservatives, and fillers.

Canned Foods

Canned, or "wet," dog foods are the most expensive commercial choices because cans and water increase shipping costs. Canned foods are better for dogs with certain medical problems or poor appetite, but a full-time diet of canned food can cause tartar buildup and gum disease, bad breath and flatulence, and large, soft, smelly stools. Nor are canned foods the most convenient, because open cans must be refrigerated to prevent spoilage, and empty cans increase the volume of garbage created by feeding your dog.

Special-Formula Commercial Foods

What about all of those "special-formula" dog foods you see advertised for puppies, seniors, small dogs, big dogs, active dogs, fat dogs, and on and on? If you compare labels, many of these "specialized" formulas are nearly, if not completely, identical to other commercial formulas. Even where they differ to some extent, their "special benefits" are often debatable, and some

may hurt your dog's health. For example, few dogs need the extra calories and protein found in "active" foods, and most knowledgeable breeders and vets prefer to feed puppies a high-quality maintenance food rather than a higher-calorie "puppy formula" that pushes growth too quickly.

In contrast, some specialized foods do benefit dogs with specific health problems, such as kidney problems. Some of these are available only through veterinarians, while others are more widely available, including a number of foods designed for dogs with certain food sensitivities. Many of these foods use no preservatives or fillers, and they often replace commonly used grains and meats with such less-common alternatives.

Noncommercial Diets

If you want to control the ingredients that go into your Brittany's diet, if you don't mind shopping for and preparing the food, and if you have room to store the ingredients and prepared foods properly, then a homemade canine diet of high-quality meats, eggs, cooked vegetables, fruits, dairy products, and possibly grains may appeal to you. Detailed information on canine nutrition is beyond the scope of this book, but a number of books and websites offer sound information and recipes for properly balanced home-

Many people add dried and fresh fruits to a raw diet.

cooked meals and treats. Let's look at the basic options.

Raw Diets

Many people firmly believe that a raw canine diet is most natural. Typically, such a diet consists of raw meaty chicken and turkey bones, with additional organ meat (liver, kidney, heart, brain, tongue, and tripe) and eggs from time to time, as well as green leafy vegetables, which must be run though a food processor or juicer first. Most people also add some combination of vegetable oils, brewer's yeast, kelp, apple cider vinegar, fresh and dried fruits, and/or raw honey. Some people also add occasional small servings of grains and dairy products, especially raw goat milk, cottage cheese, and plain yogurt. Some also add vitamin and mineral supplements.

Simply feeding "natural" food to your dog is not enough to ensure that the diet is in fact balanced and complete, of course, so if you choose to go this route, be sure to consult reliable sources of information on canine nutrition and design a diet that includes a wide variety of foods and supplements in the proper proportions. Remember that you will need time to prepare your dog's food every day, no matter how busy you are. You will need proper storage facilities for ingredients and prepared meals to prevent spoilage, and you must be fastidious about cleanup. Raw meats and poultry especially can contain bacteria and sometimes parasites that can attack both your dog and your human family. You also need to be aware that cooked bones aren't the only ones that can splinter; raw bones, too, especially poultry bones, can produce shards that can injure or kill your Brittany.

Homemade Diets

If you want to control the ingredients that go into your Brittany's diet, you may choose to make home-cooked doggy meals from fresh ingredients in your own kitchen. I'm not talking about a random diet of table scraps but a carefully balanced regimen of high-quality meats, eggs, cooked vegetables, fruits, dairy products, and sometimes grains. Such a diet, when based on sound nutrition, can prevent some of the problems associated with certain ingredients in some commercial dog foods, including allergies and digestive issues.

Before you leap to this option, keep in mind that you must be committed to shopping for ingredients and preparing the food, and you must have room to store the ingredients and prepared foods properly to maintain their freshness and quality. A thorough discussion of canine nutrition is beyond the scope of this book, but a number of books and websites offer recipes for home-cooked meals and treats, or you can develop your own recipes based on your study of canine nutrition. If in doubt, ask your veterinarian for advice.

When to Feed Your Brittany

Most dogs are opportunistic eaters— they will eat whenever they have the opportunity. For wild carnivores, it's a great idea to eat when you can because it may be a while before you catch your next meal. Our companion dogs, though, rarely suffer from lack of meals—in fact, obesity is a much bigger health threat for most American dogs than is malnutrition. In any case, your Brittany's feeding schedule is up to you. Let's look at some options.

Free Feeding

Many people think that dogs who have access to food all the time won't overeat. Not true! Some free-fed dogs do stay slim , especially when they are young, but many pets who have constant access to food become obese. Ironically, others become finicky eaters because food that is always available becomes less interesting.

Free feeding, athough it seems like an easy option, can have some other drawbacks as well. If your Brittany is prone to resource guarding or aggression, free feeding can make the problem worse because your dog may forget that you control his food. Lack of a regular meal schedule will make housetraining more difficult and elimination in a trained dog less predictable. The first sign that a dog is ill is often lack of appetite, which you may not notice for a while if you free feed your dog. Finally, food left out can attract rodents, insects, and even other predators. The only logical reason to free feed a dog is to save a few minutes a day,

HOW TO READ A DOG FOOD LABEL

To make sense of dog food labels, you need to know the lingo. Here's a guide to the basics.

- **Alpha tocopherol:** Vitamin E, a natural preservative
- **Animal fat:** Fat obtained from the tissue of mammals and/or poultry in the commercial process of rendering or extracting
- **Beef tallow:** Fat from tissue of cattle
- **Brewer's rice:** Small bits of rice broken off from larger kernels of milled rice
- **Brewer's yeast:** Dried, nonfermentive by-product of brewing of beer and ale
- **Brown rice:** Unpolished rice left after kernels have been removed
- **Chicken:** Flesh and skin, with or without bone, without feathers, heads, feet, or entrails
- **Chicken by-product meal:** Ground, rendered, clean poultry parts, including necks, feet, undeveloped eggs, and intestines
- **Chicken fat:** Fat from tissue of chicken
- **Chicken meal:** Dry ground clean combination of chicken flesh and skin with or without bones
- **Dehydrated chicken:** Dried fresh chicken flesh (without skin, bones, feathers, heads, feet, or entrails)
- **Dried beet pulp:** Residue after sugar is removed from sugar beets (used as filler)
- **Fish meal:** Dried ground tissue of undecomposed whole fish or fish cuttings, which may or may not have oil removed
- **Meat:** Flesh of slaughtered animals, including muscle, tongue, diaphragm, heart, esophagus, overlying fat, skin, sinew, nerves, and blood vessels
- **Meat by-products:** Clean nonmeat parts of slaughtered animals, including lungs, spleen, kidneys, brain, liver, blood, bone, stomach, and intestines (does not include hair, horns, teeth, or hooves)
- **Poultry by-products:** Nonmeat parts of slaughtered poultry, such as heads, feet, and internal organs (does not include feathers)

and really, if you don't have time to feed your dog twice a day, you don't have time for a dog at all.

Scheduled Feeding

Feeding on a schedule has many advantages. It gives you better control of your Brittany's food intake and weight, and you will know immediately if he stops eating. Scheduled meals make housetraining easier because regular meals result in regular elimination. If you use food for training rewards, your dog will find them more interesting if he can't grab a snack whenever he wants to. In fact, with scheduled meals you consistently reinforce your image in your dog's eyes as the source of all things good—like supper!—and that will strengthen the bond between you and your dog.

Water, though, should always be available to your dog, with a few exceptions. When you are housetraining, you should limit water your dog's water for an hour or two before bedtime to reduce the number of nighttime outings (or accidents). For certain veterinary procedures, especially those requiring anesthesia, your veterinarian will require that you withhold water for a certain period. Otherwise, be sure cool clean water is always available for your dog.

Brittanys tend to be active dogs, but they can still gain weight.

Slim and Trim or Roly Poly?

Although they tend to be very active dogs, I've seen some pretty chubby Brittanys. Excess weight in dogs, as in people, has been linked to heart disease, diabetes, pancreatitis, respiratory problems, orthopedic problems, and arthritis. Besides, those extra pounds (kg) around his middle will cause your dog to overheat and tire more easily. It will also limit his ability to enjoy life as the athlete he should be and will probably cause him to die younger than he would if you kept him at a proper weight.

How can you tell whether your Brittany's weight is appropriate? One way, of course, is to weigh him, but that will tell you only whether he's gaining or losing weight, not whether his weight is appropriate. To figure that out, place your thumb on one side of your Brittany's spine and your index finger on the other just behind his shoulders and then slowly move your fingers along his spine toward his tail. With only light downward pressure, you should be able to feel the ribs attached to the vertebrae. Next, look down on your dog's back while he's standing. You should see a distinct "waist" where his body narrows slightly between his ribs and his hips. If you can't feel ribs or see a

waist, your Brittany needs to go on a diet.

If your Brittany has turned into a chunky monkey, don't panic, but do take steps to get him back in shape. Here are some tips for doggy dieters:

- Remember that the feeding guidelines for most commercial dog foods suggest more food than the average dog needs. If your dog is fat, he needs less food, no matter what the bag says.
- Use a standard measuring utensil to measure the amount you feed your dog. If you use a scoop or mug or something else to dish up the food, there's a good chance that you are feeding your dog more than you think you are.
- To take weight off your dog, you must reduce his caloric intake. Most dogs will overeat whenever possible, so it's up to you to control your Brittany's food and weight.

If your Brittany has eaten his allotment of calories and you really think he's still hungry, you can add bulk without calories. One way is to take a meal's worth of dry food, divide it in two, and soak one half in water for a half hour or so, letting it absorb water and expand. Then mix the dry portion into the soaked portion and serve. The swollen kibble will take up more room in your dog's stomach, making him feel as if he has eaten more food. Another trick is to mix high-fiber, low-calorie food into

Check It Out

FEEDING CHECKLIST

To keep your Brittany in the best possible health:

- ✓ Feed a balanced diet.
- ✓ Choose high-quality foods, whether commercial or homemade.
- ✓ Provide plenty of clean water.
- ✓ Keep your dog at a healthy weight.
- ✓ Exercise your Brittany every day.

your dog's regular food—some foods that work well include the following: unsalted green beans (uncooked fresh beans or frozen beans are fine; canned beans should be rinsed thoroughly to remove salt); lettuce or raw spinach; canned pumpkin (not pie filling, just plain pumpkin); or unsalted, air-popped popcorn (but not if your Brittany is allergic to corn).

Reduced-calorie dog foods sometimes work but usually are not necessary and are often not effective. All too many dogs remain chubby on long-term diets of "light" food because they still eat too much.

Remember that treats and snacks add to the day's intake—feeding less dog food or using a diet dog food won't help if your dog also gets all sorts of other goodies. Set aside part of your dog's daily food allowance to use as rewards—it's amazing how wonderful most dogs find a single piece of plain old dog food. Or

use low-calorie goodies; small bits of raw carrot or green bean, or sugar-free oat cereal, works well.

In addition to controlling your Brittany's food intake, make sure that he is getting enough exercise. Brittanys are bred to run long distances in the field, and daily exercise is critical for good physical health. Not only will it help keep him slim and trim, but it will also tone his muscles, build strong bones, maintain his joints, and help keep his cardiovascular and immune systems healthy. The big bonus? Exercise will also improve your dog's behavior by directing his energy into acceptable activities and preventing boredom.

Age, exercise, general health, and other factors all affect your dog's dietary needs, so it's important to modify his food intake and exercise as his needs change to keep him healthy and happy throughout his life.

Chapter
5

Grooming Your Brittany

Although Brittanys are not high maintenance compared to many other breeds, you do need to groom your dog regularly to keep him looking and feeling his best. Keeping your dog groomed will also cut down on dog-related housework by minimizing hair on floors and furniture and preventing scratched floors and snagged carpets and upholstery. Let's begin with an inventory of the grooming supplies you need and then see how to use them.

Grooming Supplies

Using the right tools to groom your Brittany will make the job a lot easier. You don't need a lot of tools, and you don't need to purchase top-of-the-line quality for your pet, but I would recommend that you buy well-made products of reasonable quality. They will work better and last longer, saving you money in the long run. If you buy good-quality tools and take care of them, most will last at least the life of your dog. Now let's see what you need.

- **Electric clippers** with #10 blade (optional).
- **Flea comb**, which has very closely spaced metal teeth designed to trap and remove fleas from the coat.
- **Nail clippers** are essential for keeping your dog's nails a healthy length. Clippers come in two main styles: the guillotine and the scissors. The guillotine-style clipper has an opening which you slip over the nail and a blade that slides across the opening, cutting the nail from one side. A scissors-style clipper has two blades that cross in a scissors action, cutting the nail from both sides. Which style you use is matter of personal preference. Either way, check frequently to be sure the moving parts are working properly and that the blades are sharp. Dull blades and misaligned or loose working parts can hurt your dog when you clip his nails.
- **Natural bristle brush** for smoothing the coat.

Buy well-made products to groom your Brittany.

- **Pin brush**, which normally is a plastic or wooden handle with metal or plastic pins, sometimes with ball ends to protect the dog's skin.
- **Scissors**, ideally designed for cutting hair.
- **Shampoo**. You'll find all sorts of fancy schmancy dog shampoos on the shelves, but all you really need is a mild shampoo formulated for dogs. (People shampoos will dry out your dog's skin and coat.) Your dog's sense of smell is much more sensitive than yours, so don't overpower him with strong fragrances. Avoid medicated and flea shampoos unless your vet advises you to use them.
- **Slicker brush**, which is similar to a pin brush but with shorter metal pins usually set close together.
- **Smoothing tool** to smooth nails. Emery boards made for acrylic nails are inexpensive and work well on canine nails. Many people prefer to use a portable electric-powered rotary mechanism equipped with a sandpaper drum to grind the nail instead of clipping or to smooth the edges after clipping. Dremel is a popular brand of this tool.
- **Styptic powder** (or small bag of cornstarch) to stop bleeding if you cut a nail too short and it bleeds.
- **Thinning shears** for thinning out thick patches of thick fur and for trimming without leaving distinct scissors lines.

Both scissors and thinning sheers are available in any beauty supply store.
- **Tooth care products** designed specifically for dogs, including toothpaste and a toothbrush or substitute tooth-cleaning device.

You may want to use a plastic box with a lid to keep your grooming supplies organized and easy to pack if you and your dog decide to hit the road.

Brushing

Compared to many other breeds, your Brittany doesn't require a lot of brushing to keep his coat clean and healthy, but he does need to be brushed thoroughly two or three times a week. A multi-purpose activity, a good brushing:
- removes loose hair, debris, and dirt from the coat
- distributes natural skin oils that lubricate hair and make it shine
- cuts down on house cleaning (and yes, Brittanys do shed)
- enhances the bond between you and your dog as you focus on one another
- gives you an opportunity to check your dog for lumps, bumps, and other booboos
- keeps your Brittany looking his best day in and day out

How to Brush

Use your pin brush to brush the hair on your dog's body, stroking with the direction

CUTTING THE NAILS TOO SHORT

Q: "What should I do if I cut my dog's nail too short and make it bleed?"

A: "If you accidentally cut a little too much nail and cause it to bleed, dip the nail into a little styptic powder (available from pet supply and drug stores) or corn starch," advises professional groomer Andrea Cole. "The bleeding should stop very quickly. If you have cut way too short and the bleeding doesn't stop within two or three minutes, apply pressure to the nail with a clean cloth. If it still doesn't stop in a few minutes, call your veterinarian."

of growth. Your slicker brush will work well to keep his feathering tangle-free and clean. If the hair is tangled, begin toward the bottom of each section of hair and brush out to the end, removing tangles as you go. Work your way up the section until you are able to brush easily from the roots to the ends. If you have a natural bristle brush, finish up by using it to smooth your dog's coat in the direction of growth. Voilà! Your Brittany is brushed!

Bathing

Gather all of your supplies before you start. You don't want a wet dog and no towels! Brush your dog to remove loose hair before you wet him, and if he has any tangles or mats in his feathers, remove them while they're dry. You need to protect your dog's inner ears from water and his eyes from soap. You can gently place a cotton ball into the opening of each ear, and you can apply ophthalmic ointment (available from your vet, groomer, or pet supply store) to his eyes. If you don't take those precautions, then be very careful not to squirt water into his ears or get soap in his eyes, as either can cause long-term problems.

How to Bathe

Get your dog into the tub and reward him, then wet him with lukewarm (not hot) water. Apply a mild dog shampoo and gently work it into his fur, beginning at his neck and working toward his tail. Repeat with his chest and belly, up under his hind legs, and under his tail. Don't lather his face; instead, use a washcloth to wash it gently and a clean one to remove shampoo.

If you're trying to kill fleas, wet and lather your dog thoroughly, beginning with a "collar" of lather high on his neck to keep any fleas from leaving his body to hide in his ears. You don't need insecticidal shampoo; regular shampoo left on for about ten minutes to drown the fleas will do the trick.

Shampoo residue can irritate your dog's skin and leave his fur sticky, so it's essential to rinse him thoroughly. Then run your hands all over his body to be sure that you got all the soap, which will feel slick and leave bubbles on your hand if it's there. Soap loves to hide in doggy armpits, the groin, and the groove along the belly between the ribs, so check those areas carefully. When the shampoo is out, gently squeeze the excess water from your dog's coat. Then gently pat out as much moisture as possible with a towel or two.

Before bathing your Brittany, brush him to remove tangles or mats.

Praise and reward your dog for being so good before you release him, then carefully let him go so that he doesn't hurt himself or something else with a wild leap. It's usually smart to put on a collar and leash before releasing a wet dog from a tub to prevent him from running and rolling and rubbing himself on your carpets, walls, furniture, bedspreads—or if you're outdoors, dirt.

If your Brittany has a very straight, flat coat, you can let him air-dry, or you can speed the process with a force dryer made for dogs or a regular hair dryer set on cool. If his coat is wavy or thick, you may want to blow him dry.

Trimming

Your Brittany may benefit from a little trimming of his feet, ears, neck, and other areas from time to time to remove straggly long hairs. Such trimming improve your dog's appearance and can also help keep him healthier and cleaner. To learn the finer points of trimming a Brittany, contact your local breed club or kennel club to find out about grooming workshops or to find someone who can teach you. In the meantime, you can get started here. Just remember, when trimming, take your time and be careful not to cut your dog's skin— or your own!

How to Trim the Feet

Long hair growing from between your dog's toes can be trimmed to keep it from

PUPPY TEETH

If your Brittany is a puppy, check his mouth and teeth every few days. Puppies, like human babies, are born toothless. Their deciduous, or baby, teeth come in at about four weeks. Permanent teeth will replace the baby teeth when your pup is between three and five months old. (See also "Destructive Chewing" in Chapter 7.) Sometimes the permanent tooth fails to push the baby tooth out. If not removed, the retained tooth will cause the permanent teeth to be misaligned, keep the jaw bones from developing properly, and cause pain. If you think that your pup has retained a baby tooth, take him to your vet.

collecting plant matter, stones, ice, and other debris and to keep it from making him slip on smooth surfaces. Besides, a neatly trimmed foot looks nicer. Here's how to trim your dog's feet:

- Using straight (not thinning) shears, trim the hair on the underside of the foot so that it is even with the pads.
- Using a slicker brush, brush the hair from between the toes and from the top of the foot against the growth so that it stands up; using thinning shears or straight shears, trim the hair to a consistent short length on top of the foot. Don't trim between the toes—that will give your dog a splay-footed look.
- Trim any long hair around the dewclaw.
- Comb the hair on the back of the pastern (the area between the foot and the long bone of the leg) against the grain, then trim it to about 1/2 (1.5 cm) inch.

- According to the American Kennel Club (AKC) breed standard, the feathers on your Brittany's hind legs should reach "halfway to the hocks" (the joint above the long, vertical leg bone). If they are longer than that, or straggly, use thinning sheers to shorten and tidy them. Snip judiciously so that the feathers look natural rather than "bobbed." You can also trim any long hairs on or above the hocks as well.
- The feathers on your dog's front legs should be about 2 to 4 inches (5 to 10 cm) long. As with the rear feathers, you can tidy them with thinning shears. Trim the long hair but try not to get a straight, artificial edge. Toward the bottom of the leg, taper the feathers to about 1 inch (2.5 cm).
- The featherings along your Brittany's underside should hang only 1 or 2 inches (2.5 or 5 cm) below the elbow

and can be trimmed with thinning shears. Again, try not to create an artificially sharp, straight line; take tiny snips and then stand back and look until you get the appearance you want.

How to Trim the Tail

Your Brittany's tail may take on an unkempt appearance without trimming, but it's easy to keep that from happening. To tidy up the tail:

- Trim any straggly hairs from the tip, so that it looks neat and rounded.
- Comb or brush the hair on the underside of the tail against the growth, then trim so that the hair is even with the tail's underside.
- Finish with thinning shears and a very light hand—tidy up any stray hairs, but don't overtrim the tail.
- If your dog grows long hair below the base of his tail, you can use your scissors to trim the area, which will help keep it clean.

How to Trim the Neck

Some Brittanys grow a lot of hair on their necks, and if it's curly or wavy, it can make their necks look thick. If you prefer a tidier look, you can trim the hair on the front and sides of your dog's neck from the ears to just abve the sternum, using scissors or clippers. Getting the neck to look good, though, can be tricky. The best way to learn is to have a knowledgeable Brittany breeder or owner, or groomer, show you how; if you plan to show your Brittany in conformation, this is essential.

The simplest trim for pets and hunting dogs consists of removing long hair from behind your dog's ears and down the sides of the neck. You can use scissors, or clippers with a number 10 blade and, ideally, with a comb attachment to keep you from cutting the hair too short. Clip in the direction of the hair's growth, not against it. If your dog has not been clipped before, give him time to get used to the sound of the clippers before you try to use them. Take several sessions if necessary, and reward him with a good treat for tolerating the noise.

How to Trim the Ears

Your dog's ears—actually, the ear leathers, or floppy part—may also get a little shaggy looking if you don't tidy them up occasionally. Use your thinning shears to avoid sharp cut lines, and carefully trim along the outside edges of the ears. If your dog has a lot of long hair on the underside of the ear flap, you can trim that as well.

Nail Care

Far too many dogs have excessively long nails. Please don't let your dog be one of them! Overgrown nails that hit the ground with every step force the toes out of their normal position and distort the foot. Eventually this can lead to lameness

If you choose to use a rotary grinder for your Brittany's nails, have a professional demonstrate how to use it properly.

and permanent deformity. Besides, nicely trimmed nails are less likely to scratch floors or snag carpets or upholstery. If you hear the click of nails when your dog walks on a hard surface, it's time for a pedicure.

Nail trimming doesn't have to be an ordeal for you or your dog if you take some time to do it right. Begin by teaching your Brittany that having his feet handled is no big deal. When you're hanging out with your dog, hold each of his feet one at a time and gently massage and flex his toes. If he objects, hold one foot gently and give him a treat while still holding his foot. Be sure that you reward him for letting you hold his foot, not for pulling it away. Do this for a few sessions without trying to trim his nails. When he's comfortable letting you hold his feet, try trimming one nail. If he doesn't fight you, go ahead and trim another. If he tries to pull away, trim just the one nail. Then give him a treat while you're still holding his foot, and then let go and pet him. Do another nail later. Continue holding his paws at various times without trimming, too. Be patient, and soon your dog will know that you aren't going to hurt him.

How to Trim the Nails

Now let's talk about how to trim the nails. Find a comfortable place and position with plenty of light. Hold your dog's paw gently but firmly, press lightly on the bottom of the footpad to extend the nail, and trim it below the quick (which is the living part of the nail). If your dog has light-colored nails, the quick will look pink from the blood vessels inside it. If his nails are dark, cut below where the nail narrows and curves downward. After you trim the tip, look at the end of the nail. If you see a black dot near the center, you're at the quick and it's time to stop trimming. If not, shave a little more off and check again. If your dog cooperates, do all of his nails, including the dewclaws, the little toes inside his legs above his front feet. If he's not yet used to having his nails trimmed, go back to basic nail training as described earlier. Keep your nail clippers sharp, and be sure that they are properly aligned. Dull or poorly aligned blades won't cut cleanly, and they pinch.

Clippers often leave sharp rough edges on nails, making them prone to snagging and scratching. If you like, you can smooth your dog's nails with a few short downward strokes of an inexpensive emery board (the kind made for acrylic nails work well) or with a sandpaper drum on a Dremel tool, which is a rotary grinder. Although Dremels are not difficult to use, they do get hot, and long hair can easily get caught and wrapped tight about the rotating drum, so it's a good idea to have someone with experience show you how to use the tool safely and effectively.

If you prefer not to trim your dog's nails yourself, you can have your groomer or vet do it for you. Just be sure that you take your Brittany in regularly, which is every three to four weeks for most dogs.

Ear Care

Allergies, hormonal problems, and excess moisture can all promote abnormal growth of yeast or bacteria in your dog's moist, warm ear canal, leading to painful infections. Dirt, plant matter, and various parasites like fleas, ticks, and mites can also inhabit doggy ears and cause problems. So clearly it's important to check your Brittany's ears at least once a week.

What does a healthy ear look like? The skin inside the ear should be pink or flesh colored, not red or inflamed. You should not see large globs of wax or dirty-looking discharge or smell strong or nasty odors. If your dog scratches or rubs his head or ears a lot, shakes or tilts his head, or cries or pulls away when you touch his ears or the area around them, he may also have an infection or other problem.

How to Care for the Ears

Don't treat ear problems without veterinary advice. To treat an infection effectively, it must be accurately diagnosed.

GROOMING CHECKLIST

- ✓ The right tools make grooming a snap.
- ✓ Brush your Brittany two or three times a week.
- ✓ Teach your dog to accept the occasional bath without a fight.
- ✓ Trim your dog's nails every three to four weeks or as needed.

- ✓ Check your dog's ears at least once a week.
- ✓ Report changes in your dog's eyes to your vet.
- ✓ Make dental care part of your dog's health-care routine.

Inappropriate treatment will prolong your dog's discomfort and may also cause more damage, making the infection more difficult to treat later.

If your dog's ears are dirty but not inflamed or sensitive, you can clean them with a mild cleanser designed for canines. Ask your vet for a recommendation, and follow the directions on the product. Do it outdoors or in a bathroom or other area you can clean easily—most dogs shake their heads after ear cleanser is applied, flinging cleaner and wax far and wide. When both ears are cleaned and shaken, gently wipe them with a cotton ball or tissue. *Never* push anything into your dog's ear canals; you could damage the ear drums and cause deafness. If your Brittany has very waxy ears or if he does things that get his ears wet, clean them about once a week. If his ears stay nice and clean on their own, you don't need to do anything except check them regularly.

Eye Care

Healthy eyes are clear and moist. If your dog's eyes show signs of redness, swelling, or squinting, or excess tearing or mucus, take your dog to the vet. Those abnormalities could be signs of infection, abrasion, or some other potentially serious problem.

How to Care for the Eyes

You can also do a few things at home to protect your Brittany's eyes and help keep them healthy into old age. First, keep the area around your dog's eyes clean. Mucus left in the corners of the eyes can harbor bacteria, so gently wipe the corners once or twice a day with a moist washcloth or tissue. When you travel with your dog, keep him away from open windows—debris or insects hitting at the speed of a car can cause serious, painful injury to delicate eyes. When you groom your dog, be careful to keep soap and other chemicals out of his eyes.

As your Brittany enters his senior years, his eyes may appear cloudy for any of several reasons. Most common is nuclear sclerosis, an age-related change in the lens that usually does not impair vision. Clouding may also indicate a cataract, which can cause partial or complete vision loss. Tell your veterinarian if you see changes in your dog's eyes.

Dental Care

Gum disease develops when bacteria and food particles collect along the gum line and form plaque, which in turn forms tartar (calculus), irritating the gums and leading to gingivitis (inflammation of the gum) and periodontal disease. The end result is not just the notorious "dog breath" suffered by owners of dogs with poor dental care but also abscesses, infections, and loss of teeth and bone. Such oral infections also contribute to heart, liver, and kidney disease. Luckily, they are preventable.

How to Care for the Teeth

In a perfect world, you would brush your dog's teeth every day to remove the plaque. Realistically, doing so even every few days will prevent most tartar from forming. Don't use "people toothpaste" on your dog—it's not made to be swallowed and will upset your dog's stomach. Ask your vet to recommend a toothpaste made for dogs. You can apply the toothpaste with a canine toothbrush that is designed to fit the canine mouth, a finger brush (a plastic device that fits onto your finger), or even a piece of surgical gauze wrapped around your finger. Gently brush or rub your dog's teeth and gums to begin the cleaning process; enzymes in the toothpaste continue cleaning after you finish. Start slowly, and always make the process pleasant for your dog. If you're unsure, or if you have trouble brushing your dog's teeth, ask your vet to demonstrate the proper technique. Make sure that dental checkups are part of your Brittany's routine veterinary care.

Brushing your dog's teeth will prevent most tartar from forming.

Chapter
6

Training
Your Brittany

Brittanys are intelligent, energetic, determined, and joyful dogs. Those traits make them outstanding companions if you give them direction and benevolent leadership, but those same traits can also make owning a Brittany a challenge. And that's where training comes in.

Basic obedience training will give your dog a foundation for all learning. When accomplished with kindness and positive motivation, training will teach your Brittany to do what you want and avoid doing what you don't want. It will also confirm that you are in charge and that you will provide your dog with safety, leadership, and all the good things in life. The security that comes with that knowledge will help your dog be a better companion.

Positive Training for Positive Results

Imagine if you signed up to learn a new skill and your instructor yelled and punished you every time you made a mistake and never bothered to tell you when you did something well. How happy would you be, and how well would you learn? Now imagine that your teacher encourages and praises you for small improvements and really cheers you on when you improve a lot. Which teacher would you prefer? Now be that teacher for your Brittany. He will learn more

quickly, and he will trust you. Harsh punishments—hitting, kicking, leash jerking, and so on—have no place in a healthy human/dog relationship. Such methods will take the joy out of training for both of you. Training with positive motivation, like treats and praise, is more effective and more humane than training done by intimidation.

Ideally, you will enroll your Brittany in at least one obedience class based on positive reinforcement training methods. In addition, you will need to reinforce what you and your dog learn in class by training out of class. Remember, your dog is always learning from you, so take advantage of opportunities as they arise at home or out and about. We can touch on only the basics here, so in addition to taking a class, consider reading at least one book on positive training (such as my book *Training Your Dog for Life*). Above all, be patient with your dog. Learning is hard work, so help him master the lessons.

Socialization

Socialization is the process of becoming familiar with the world and its residents. Ideally, dogs experience lots of socializing experiences during their first two years. Especially important is the period between about 7 and 16 weeks of age, when puppies form many lifelong impressions and attitudes. In fact, a dog who is not socialized as a puppy is likely to be afraid of the unfamiliar as an adult. He may respond by cowering, hiding, running or trying to run away, or by displaying extremely submissive behavior, such as urination. Some dogs respond to fear and anxiety by becoming aggressive. People often assume, based on fearful behavior, that adopted dogs have been abused, but in many cases the dogs simply were not taught about the world.

How to Socialize

If your Brittany is a puppy, begin socializing him as soon as possible. Do ask your vet's advice about exposure to other animals if your pup hasn't had all of his vaccinations, but don't postpone safe socialization. Once your pup passes the critical 16-week mark, you can't get that time back. Make the effort—the results will be worth it for the rest of your dog's life. If you have an older Brittany who missed out on puppy socialization, you may not completely make up for what he's missed, but you can improve his comfort by socializing and training him.

To become properly socialized, your Brittany needs to meet lots of people—men, women, old, young, bald, hairy, with and without glasses. He also needs to

A properly socialized Brittany will be able to get along well with other dogs.

THE CRATE

Q: Isn't it mean to lock my dog in a crate?

A: "Your puppy will form an association with the crate depending on how you use it," says professional dog trainer Clarice Kashuba. "If you use it as a punishment, he will dread the crate. If you introduce the crate as a place for treats and praise and quiet time, it will fulfill your puppy's instinctual desire for a den. It will become his safe haven, and he will enjoy going there at times throughout his life."

experience different kinds of places and to walk on all sorts of surfaces. The sooner he learns to accept variations in his environment, the sooner he will become more comfortable when faced with the unfamiliar.

To be fully socialized and able to interact appropriately with others of his own species, your Brittany also needs to interact with other dogs. Regardless of your dog's age, he's potentially vulnerable to disease or injury, of course, so use good judgment about the dogs he meets, but do try to arrange for him to meet good-tempered, well-cared-for dogs. Not only will he learn to communicate with and understand his own kind, but he'll be happier. Remember, dogs are social animals, and healthy, well-socialized dogs enjoy interacting with their own kind.

Your dog should also be socialized to other types of animals that he may encounter. If you have cats or other small pets, introduce them to your dog slowly and carefully. Always make the safety of both animals your first concern.

Crate Training

If your Brittany is a puppy or an adult who isn't completely reliable or comfortable when left alone in the house, using a crate will keep him and your other belongings safer. If you are housetraining your dog, a crate used properly will speed the process. Remember, though, that your dog's crate should be his safe place, a pleasant refuge, so don't use a crate for punishment, don't push your dog in or yell as you put him in, and don't keep him locked up for excessive periods. If you follow those simple guidelines, chances are your Brittany will enter his crate willingly when you ask him to and even go there on his own when he wants to get away from it all.

How to Crate Train

If your Brittany has never been in a crate, it may take him a few days to accept the idea. To help him accept it, don't turn your dog's crate into solitary confinement. Place it in a well-traveled part of the house so that he feels that he's part of the family even when he can't run loose. When you're not home, he will still have the reassurance of your scent around him. To give the crate positive associations, feed your dog there for a while. At other times, toss in a treat or a special chew toy and say "Crate!" or "Kennel!" as he follows it in. Don't always close the door when he goes in, and when you do close it, give him another small treat.

Vary the amount of time your dog is in the crate with the door latched. When you're at home, close the door sometimes for only a minute or two. When you need to leave him there longer, give him a special chew toy that he gets only when in his crate. This will reinforce the idea that good things happen in his crate, and he won't associate it only with long periods of being locked in. And don't make a big deal out of letting him out of the crate—that will only make him think that getting out of the crate is good, so getting into the crate must be not so good. When your dog is playing outside the crate, leave the door open so that he can go in if he wants to. My adult dogs often lie in their crates with the doors wide open.

If possible, put the crate in your bedroom at night. For one thing, if you're housetraining your dog, you'll hear him if he needs to go out during the night. More importantly, sleeping where he can hear and smell you will reinforce your dog's sense of family (or pack) and strengthen the bond between you.

Housetraining

Most people agree that learning not to eliminate in the house is vital. Happily, most Brittanys learn fairly quickly where they should and shouldn't go,

Puppies do not have full bladder control until they are several months old.

but remember that individuals vary a bit. Some get the idea with nary an accident; others take a little longer. Either way, it's your job to help your dog learn the rules and to make it easy for him to follow them.

Healthy dogs raised in clean environments like to be clean. Remember, though, that puppies do not have full bladder or bowel control until they are several months old. If you have a Brittany puppy, be patient, and try to anticipate your puppy's needs. He will need to urinate and defecate shortly after he wakes up, during or shortly after meals, and during or after exercise. Younger puppies go more frequently.

Crates work well for housetraining because most dogs do not like to soil their sleeping space. But your dog's perception of that space is different from your perception, and if your puppy is in an adult-sized crate, he may be happy to piddle at one end, then snooze 30 inches (76 cm) away. For that reason, until he is housetrained, your dog's crate should be only large enough for him to stand up, turn around, and lie down. If he's a puppy in an adult-sized crate, that's fine—just block part of the crate to limit his usable space.

How to Housetrain

Always watch your puppy or untrained adult dog closely when he's loose in the house. If he starts to sniff the floor, circle, or arch his back, take him out immediately. If he's a young puppy, he may not have much physical control, so pick him up and carry him out. If you want him to learn to use a specific place for his business, take him there on leash and stay with him until he finishes.

You can teach your dog to go "on command"—very useful at times! When he starts to go, tell him "Go potty" or "Hurry up." When he finishes, praise him in a happy voice, and give him a small treat or a short playtime. Don't reward him until he's finished eliminating—keep him focused on the job at hand so that he learns not to dawdle. Do this consistently for awhile and he will learn to associate your words with his act; you'll be able to take him out and tell him what to do, and he will.

If you are housetraining your dog and he doesn't do his business within ten minutes of being taken outdoors, take him in and crate him for 10 to 15 minutes. Then go out and try again. Until you are sure that you know your dog's elimination patterns, wait a few minutes before you take him back in. Some dogs do not completely empty their bladders or bowels on the first attempt. Keep in mind that your goal is to prevent accidents as much as possible. A few extra minutes spent in the training stage can save you time, money, cleanups, and frustration throughout the rest of your dog's life. Some health problems can make control difficult or impossible, so if you are diligent about supervision and training and your dog is still having regular accidents at six months or older, speak to your veterinarian.

Dealing With Accidents

Accidents happen. Don't punish your dog—chastise yourself for giving him too much freedom in the house or too much time between breaks. Punishment (nose rubbing, hitting, yelling) will not teach your dog what you want him to do but will teach him that he shouldn't let you see him pee or poop! He won't necessarily translate that to mean that he should go outdoors, and you may create a long-term problem. It's much better to strive for prevention and reward success.

If you see your dog eliminating in the house, calmly take him outside. If he's a puppy, pick him up and carry him—he will nearly always stop in the middle, and putting him down in the right place to finish the job will help him understand what you want. When he finishes in the correct place, reward him and then put him into his crate or a safe confined area with a nice chewy toy so that you can clean up his booboo.

Don't punish your puppy for eliminating in the wrong place; reward him when he gets it right!

CRATING YOUR PUPPY

How long should your dog be in a crate? The generally accepted guideline is the puppy's age plus one, meaning for instance that a two-month-old puppy can probably be crated without having an accident for up to three hours. If he's six months old, up to seven hours. That's about the maximum, even if your dog can go longer than that without needing to relieve himself. Even for an adult dog, being confined to a crate for that long is tough physically and mentally except in special circumstances. If you are away from home for long hours every day, consider hiring someone to come in and take your dog out for a walk or romp every four hours or so, or take him to a safe doggy day care facility, at least until he can be safely left loose in the house during the day.

Use a good odor and stain remover made for organic waste—you can find several such products in pet supply stores. (A 50/50 solution of white vinegar and water will neutralize urine but not feces). In any case, you must remove all trace of the odor, and regular cleaners won't do that. Your Brittany has a spectacular sense of smell, and even if you can't smell urine or feces, your dog may be able to. The smell of urine or feces is like a big neon "go here" sign for him. If possible, restrict your puppy to rooms with uncarpeted flooring to make accidents easier to clean up.

If you feed your dog a high-quality diet, housetraining will be easier because he will digest his food better and have more manageable stools. If you feed him dry dog food, your dog will need access to plenty of water, but be sure to remove the water two hours before bedtime until he is fully housetrained. Finally, try to feed him at the same time every day so that you can predict when he will need to go out.

Commands That Every Brittany Should Know

In this limited space we can't explore everything your Brittany could learn, but we can look at a few basic commands that can make an enormous difference in the quality of the life you share. These simple behaviors—*sit*, *lie down*, *stay*, *come*, and *walk nicely*—will make your Brittany a pleasure to live with, keep him safer, and make both of you more confident as you go through life together. Let's start training!

The Release Word

In principle, if you give a command, your dog should obey and continue the behavior indefinitely. If you don't expect him to do so, you are essentially letting him decide how long is good enough—a minute, a second, etc. To make the duration of a command clear for your dog, you need not only the command itself but also a way to tell your dog that he's off the hook. The easiest way is to teach him a release word that means that he's no longer required to obey the previous command.

How to Teach the Release Word

Many people simply use "Okay." That's fine, but because many of us say "okay" pretty frequently, it's extremely easy to release the dog without meaning to. Many experienced trainers prefer to use a less frequently used word for the release. I use "Free."

To teach the release, combine it with other commands. For instance, teach the *sit* command as described in the next section, and after your dog sits for a few seconds, tell him "Free" (or whatever word you choose) and encourage him to get up by walking a few steps away and getting excited. Don't give him a

Lying down on command may seem pretty basic, but as with the *recall*, a lot of dogs never learn the command well enough to be reliable. This is partly because of the nature of the position itself, which many dogs view as submissive.

food reward—being released from the original command is a reward in itself. If your dog breaks the command before you use your release word, simply put him back where he's supposed to be for a few seconds, then use your release. He'll soon get the idea.

Sit

Sit is a useful command and one that most dogs learn to obey (at least when there is food in their faces!). It gives you a positive way to tell your dog to control himself when he's excited or scared, which works a lot better than frantically pleading "No, don't do that, stop it!" By telling him to sit when you think that he is about to do something you don't like, you turn a negative behavior into a positive one and reinforce him for being a good dog.

The trick, of course, is to teach your Brittany to sit when you tell him, no matter where he is or what's happening, and to remain sitting until you release him. Let's focus on getting your dog to sit and stay put every time you tell him.

How to Teach *Sit*

Start with your dog on leash or confined in a small space. Hold a treat in front of his nose, but don't let him have it. Slowly raise the treat enough to clear the top of his head, and move it back over his head toward his tail. As his nose rises to follow the treat, his rear end will go down. As he begins to fold his hind legs, tell him "Sit." When his fanny hits the floor, praise him and give him the treat. Then release him with your release word. Repeat three or four times per formal training session, and take advantage of other training opportunities throughout the day—have him sit for his dinner, before he goes out the door, before you throw his ball, and so on.

As your dog learns to respond reliably to the *sit* command, reward him only for fast responses and for holding the *sit* for longer times. Even if you don't tell him to stay (which we'll get to later), he should continue doing what you told him until you release him.

Down

Lying down on command may seem pretty basic, but as with the *recall*, a lot of dogs never learn the command well enough to be reliable. This is partly because of the nature of the position itself. Because being down on the ground indicates submission and therefore vulnerability, some dogs resist assuming that position, especially when other dogs are present. If your dog seems reluctant to lie down near other dogs, try moving away from the group to a place where he resists less. Then, over the course of several sessions, have him lie down closer to the other dogs.

Another common training issue is lack

of consistency from people. If you use *down* to mean *lie down,* as well as don't jump on Aunt Tilly and get off the couch, the word won't mean anything to your dog. Use a distinct command for each meaning.

How to Teach *Down*

Now let's teach your Brittany to lie down on command. I like to teach it from a standing position because it's faster. Start with your dog standing beside or in front of you. Hold a treat and slowly

Always use the same word to call your dog to come to you.

move your hand downward under your dog's chin, toward his front legs, lowering it as you go. As his nose follows the treat, your dog should fold back until he's lying down. If he lowers his front only, gently guide his rear end down. If he backs up without lying down, try moving your hand more slowly. If that doesn't work, hold your other arm behind him so that he can't back up. If he lowers his head but doesn't lie down, press very gently between his shoulder blades to guide him. If he still doesn't go down, keep the treat close to the ground with one hand, and cradle his hind legs from behind with the other. Gently tighten your arm around his hind legs until he folds down. As soon as he lies down, praise him and give him the treat.

When your dog begins to lie down quickly for the treat, add your command (you choose one: "down," "lie down," "settle") as you begin the downward motion. When he's responding quickly and reliably, give the command without moving your hand. When he lies down, praise and reward him (be sure to give him the treat while he's lying down, not after he gets up). Slowly increase the length of time he has to stay down before he gets the treat.

Come

How many dogs do you know who come reliably when their owners call

Check It Out

TRAINING CHECKLIST

To make life more fun for both of you:

✓ Train your Brittany using positive motivational methods rather than intimidation.

✓ Take your Brittany through at least one good obedience class.

✓ Socialize your Brittany for better mental and emotional development.

✓ Teach your dog to love his crate.

✓ Make housetraining easier through prevention and positive motivation.

✓ Teach your Brittany a few basic commands.

them? Unfortunately, too many people inadvertently teach their dogs that they don't have to come when called, leading to frustration for the owner and potential danger for the dog. But you can teach your Brittany not only to want to come when you call but also to understand that he must. Let's see how.

But first, the ground rules. Whether you are just beginning to teach a puppy or newly adopted adult, you can make your training efforts much more effective if you follow these simple guidelines:

- Always use the same word to call your dog.
- Call only once— repeating the command will teach your Brittany to ignore you. If he doesn't come when you call, go back as many steps in training as you need to.
- Be patient! Don't expect success in one or two lessons.
- Reward your dog every time he comes when called, even if the reward is just a

"Good dog" and ear scratch.

- Don't bet your Brittany's life on his response to the *come* command. Keep him on leash in unfenced areas. I know of more than one very obedient dog who was killed the one and only time he didn't come when called. Until you are about 98 percent confident that your dog will come when called, don't call him if you can't enforce the command. If you aren't sure that he will come when you call him, put him on a leash or long line for control.

- Make coming when called a wonderful thing for your Brittany. Never act angry or punish him when he comes to you. If you need to do something he doesn't care for—bath, ear cleaning, whatever—go get him rather than calling him.

- If your dog has previously learned to ignore your word for "come," find a new word and use it for retraining. "Here" is commonly used, and I have heard trainers use more unusual commands such as *By me* and *Find me*.

How to Teach *Come*

Start with your puppy or dog on leash or in a very small room or fenced area so that he's safe and can't wander away. Hold a toy he likes or a small, yummy treat. Say "Come!" *once* in a playful voice. Do whatever you have to do to get your dog to come to you—act silly, walk or run the other way, crouch down, play with the toy—but don't repeat the command. If he doesn't come on his own, gently guide him to you with the leash. When he gets to you, praise him and give him the toy or treat. Let him know how happy he's made you. Then let him return to whatever he was doing before you called. Repeat the process two or three times, then quit. Do this several times a day if possible. Soon your dog will come whenever you call!

Stay

A dog who stays is easier to live with and often safer than one who doesn't. Teaching your dog to stay on command is worth the time and effort, but teaching a reliable *stay* takes time, consistency, and patience. Don't try to rush the process—be sure that your dog is solid at each step before you take the next one, even if it's

Teaching a reliable stay takes time, consistency, and patience.

Once your Brittany knows how to walk nicely on a leash, he can make a great jogging partner.

lie down, and when he is in position, tell him "Stay." (You also can teach him a hand signal—the common signal for *stay* is the palm of the hand held briefly in front of the dog's face.) At first your dog won't understand *stay*, and he will probably start to get up. Calmly reposition your dog and tell him "Stay." When he stays down a few seconds, praise, reward, and release.

Start with very short *stays*—maybe ten seconds—and stand no more than one step from your dog. When he will stay for a solid ten seconds, you can begin to increase the length of the *stay* by very small increments—10 to 15 seconds—while you remain standing only a step away from your dog. Work slowly up to a five-minute *stay* while you stand no more than one step from your dog. When he will *stay* reliably for five minutes, add another step to your distance from him. Be prepared to put him back in position if necessary—he has to learn that this is the same exercise as before even though you are farther away. Every time you increase distance, shorten the time and then slowly build it back up. If your dog seems to be comfortable, try increasing the time by 30 seconds on each repetition. If you reach a point when he starts to fidget or to get up, shorten your distance and time by half and slowly build back up. The pattern here

only a matter of a couple of feet (m) or a few seconds. Practice *stays* in different places so that your dog learns that the *stay* means *stay* no matter where he is. Practice while you do other things— watch television, iron, cook—but don't forget that you told him to stay, and don't forget to release him.

How to Teach *Stay*

I suggest that you teach *stay* in the *down* position first because it is the easiest position for a dog to hold. Once your Brittany has learned to lie down on command, you can teach him to stay. Start with your dog on leash. Have him is increase distance, decrease time, and build back up.

The biggest mistake that people make in teaching the *stay* is to expect too much too soon. This is a stressful exercise for your dog. Give him time to learn what he's supposed to do and to trust that he'll be safe if he does. If you try to rush the process, you will spend much more time trying to correct him for not staying than you will if you simply take your time from the beginning.

Walk Nicely on Leash

All dogs should be taught basic leash skills. You should be able to take your dog for a walk around the block or into a crowded veterinary office without having your legs wrapped up or your shoulder dislocated. When he is properly leash trained, your dog will walk steadily on one side of you with the leash slack. Like many other aspects of good training, teaching him to do this will require some time and effort, but the payoff is a dog who is a pleasure to walk.

How to Teach Walk Nicely on Leash

Begin by rewarding your dog's correct behavior. Even if he's still not well behaved on leash, there will be times when he lets the leash go slack. He may even turn to look at you (probably to find out what's keeping you). The instant the leash goes slack, praise and reward your dog.

If he has already formed the habit of pulling on his leash, you need to convince him that pulling won't get him what he wants, but walking politely will make you happy enough to reward him. First, try the "no forward progress" approach: when your dog pulls, stop in your tracks. If your dog is excited, it may take him a minute, but eventually he will either stop pulling or turn and look at you. The moment the leash goes slack, praise and reward him, and then resume walking. If he pulls, stop again. You spend a few days going for short, slow walks, but most dogs figure out very quickly that pulling just doesn't work. If your Brittany pulls only when he sees something he wants—people, another dog, a squirrel—work on giving him something positive to do, such as performing a *sit* or *down* for a reward, rather than simply fighting his urge to pull toward something else.

Chapter
7

Solving Problems
With Your Brittany

Give your Brittany enough exercise to help expend his energy.

Dogs, like people, form habits. Some of these habits fit well with our human notions of good and bad canine behavior. Others we don't like so well. It doesn't take long for habits to form, but as we all know, they are hard to change. It's much easier to prevent bad habits than to eliminate them. So before we look at ways to fix those nasty bad habits, here are some steps you can take to save yourself—and your Brittany—the trouble.

- **Anticipate your dog's possible behavior.** Puppies, adolescents, and untrained adults do what comes naturally until they are taught what people expect. They chew things, they dig, they bark, they pee and poop. You're supposed to be the smarter one, so think ahead and prevent unwanted behaviors.
- **Provide an alternative to the unwanted behavior whenever possible.** It's easier to teach your dog to do *something* than to teach him to do *nothing*.
- **Evaluate your dog's motivation.** Is he responding to instinct (to look for birds in the shrubbery or to dig holes in the lawn)? Is he full of energy and bored? Is he frightened, ill, or in pain?

- **Exercise your dog's body.** A tired Brittany is a good Brittany. The amount of exercise he needs will depend to some extent on his age, overall health status, and individual energy level, but in general you should expect your Brittany to need 30 to 60 minutes of running exercise every day throughout most of his life. And that doesn't mean sending him to the backyard alone. Go out and play ball or jog with your dog! You'll both be happier and healthier.
- **Stimulate your dog's mind.** Brittanys are smart, and if you don't provide mental stimulation through training, exercise, and even puzzle toys, your dog will probably find his own mental entertainment.
- **Train your dog.** Basic obedience training will help your dog understand and trust you, which will in turn make him more secure and less likely to engage in behaviors you don't like.

If your dog already has an unwanted behavior, there are many ways to correct it without spanking, yanking, or otherwise treating your dog's mind or body with violence. Instead, motivate your dog to behave as you want him to through positive feedback such as food rewards, toys, and play. Your dog will learn more quickly and retain his trust in you, and you'll both be much happier.

Keep in mind that most behavioral problems can be solved if you're committed to finding the cause and the solution. Even better, most can be prevented completely through basic and on-going obedience training, consistency in your dog's environment, plenty of exercise, and good health care.

Now let's look at some problem behaviors and how you can fix them.

Barking (Excessive)

Dogs bark to express a wide range of meanings and emotions. It is a normal, natural behavior for dogs. Barking can be useful, giving your dog a way to alert you to a problem. Too much barking, though, can be a real problem for you and your neighbors and maybe even earn you a visit from the police.

How to Manage It

If your Brittany barks too much, be considerate of your neighbors while you work on the problem. Let them know that you're working on a solution, and don't leave your dog outdoors to bark his head off. If necessary, take him with you or to doggy day care when you're not home so he won't be a neighborhood nuisance. Then try to figure out why your dog barks too much, because an effective solution to a barking problem will depend in part on your dog's motivation.

Even if your Brittany isn't really a problem barker, teach him a *quiet* command so that you can tell him to stop

GROWLING AND SNAPPING

Q: My dog growls and snaps sometimes. How can I tell whether he's playing or showing serious aggression?

A: "Unless they are taught otherwise, it is natural for dogs to play with humans the way they play with other dogs—by barking, mouthing, and growling," says professional dog trainer Clarice Kashuba. "True aggression is more likely to surface around resources such as bones and food, not during play. Be aware of potentially aggressive body language such as tense muscles, forward ears, glaring into your eyes, and snarling. Resource guarding should never be allowed. Dogs will often go from guarding their food dish to guarding treats and random scraps of food on the floor. Some dogs will even start guarding favorite places such as the couch. Consistent training is vital to teaching your dog that you own the house, bones, dog food, etc." Kashuba, who owns Flying Colors Canine Academy in Indiana, cautions, "If you think your dog is showing aggressive tendencies, see a trainer who is experienced with such issues."

when he does bark. "Quiet" or "Enough," spoken in a normal voice, is perfect. Please don't bark "SHUT UP" at your dog—you'll be more annoying than he is! To teach *quiet*, use a treat to distract your dog from barking. When he stops barking, say "Quiet" and give him a treat. He'll soon associate the *quiet* with something yummy. As he begins to get the idea, say "Quiet" while he is barking; the instant he stops barking to look for the treat, praise him and reward him. Before long he will quiet when you ask him to.

Many dogs, especially those who are not spayed or neutered, bark to mark and defend what they perceive as their territory. This is a good thing if a burglar is prowling your yard but can get old if your dog barks at everyone who comes within range. One way to hush this type of barking is to give your dog something else to do. For instance, if he barks when the mail comes, tell him "Quiet," have him lie down, and give him a really super tasty treat. At first you may need to give him more than one treat at fairly short intervals to keep his attention on waiting for the treat. Gradually lengthen the time he has to wait for each treat until he will lie quietly while your mail is delivered. If you are consistent, he'll soon learn to lie down and lick his lips when he knows that the mail is on the way. If you learn that your dog barks to defend his territory when you aren't home, you'll need to do something to prevent the behavior from occurring. For instance, don't allow your dog access to rooms with windows he can look out.

Some dogs bark when they are afraid or anxious. In such cases, desensitization—a systematic program to reduce or eliminate the dog's fear—can make a big difference in his mental state and his behavior. Sometimes all it takes is patience and consistency on your part. For instance, if your dog is afraid of men, you can enlist the help of male dog lovers to help your dog. Carry really great treats with you, and initially ask men you meet on walks or wherever to toss treats to your dog. As he gets used to that idea, have your helpers wait until your dog is quiet before tossing the treat. Pretty soon your dog will love to see men coming his way.

Separation anxiety and other emotional problems can also lead to excessive barking and can be difficult to manage. If you suspect that your dog is suffering from a problem of this type—often reflected in other obsessive behaviors in addition to barking—and you can't manage it yourself or with a good basic obedience class, ask your vet or obedience instructor for a referral to a qualified behaviorist.

Many dogs bark to make requests. This can be a good thing —"I need to go out!" or "My water bowl is bone dry." Sometimes, though, it's a nuisance— "Gimme a cookie! Hey! Throw my ball! Hey! I'm talkin' to YOU." Although it will require some patience, the best long-term solution to demand or request barking is to completely ignore your dog when he does it. If he's used to having you obey him, he won't quit right away, but he will eventually figure out that you are no longer under his command. You can speed the process by rewarding him when he gets quiet. You can also redirect his bossy behavior by turning the tables on him—when he barks to demand something, tell him to sit or lie down or roll over, and then reward him. He'll learn

Some types of barking can be stopped with consistent training.

that giving you an order results in your giving one back.

Boredom can also lead to excessive barking, so if your Brittany barks too much, take a look at his life. Is he getting enough daily exercise? Is his mind stimulated by games, toys, exercise, long walks, and challenging training? If not, get busy. After all, the best thing about having a dog is the fun you have with him, right?

Destructive Chewing

Chewing is a natural and pleasurable behavior for dogs. When puppies are cutting teeth, they chew to relieve the discomfort, and many enjoy chewing well into adulthood. Chewing feels good, relieves stress, and uses up energy. If your dog chews the right things, his teeth and gums will stay cleaner and healthier as well.

How to Manage It

Some dogs, though, chew anything and everything, especially when they are anxious. Such indiscriminate chewing can damage property and even endanger your dog. Fortunately, you can control most destructive chewing if you are proactive and take the following steps:

- Be sure to give your Brittany basic obedience training and lots of daily exercise to use up energy and prevent boredom.
- When you're with your dog, be aware

of what he's up to. One of my dogs once lay at my feet and chewed one of the heels off a pair of my shoes while I assumed he had his Nylabone. My fault! If your dog picks up something he shouldn't have, gently take it and give him one of his own toys. Don't punish him for giving it to you—you want him to want to give you things.

- When you can't watch him, confine your dog with one or two good safe chew toys or bones to keep him busy.

PREVENTING PROBLEMS

Puppies are information sponges, soaking up everything you teach them. To prevent long-term problem behaviors with your adult Brittany, teach your puppy what you want from the start through careful management and training. Prevent him from forming bad habits and motivate him through positive obedience training methods—he will grow up to be the dog of your dreams.

A room without temptations may work, but a crate is often a safer choice.

- Be patient and teach your dog what's right and what isn't. The difference between your new leather handbag and a rawhide toy may be obvious to you, but it's all nice chewy leather to your dog. Put anything you don't want chewed out of reach (as I should have done with my shoes!).

Digging

Dogs dig for many reasons: to find things, to hide things, to tunnel under or out, to create a nice "bed" in the soil. Some dig because they're bored, and some dig just for fun. Unfortunately, you may not see the same joy in your dog's digging as he does. But how can you stop him?

How to Manage It

As with many other unwanted but natural doggy behaviors, your best solution is proactive management. You'll have to plan ahead a bit, but if your dog likes to dig and you don't want a moonscape for a yard, you have to do something. Here are some ideas:

- Supervise your dog whenever he's outdoors. That works for some people, but for most of us it's just not practical all the time, so you may need to combine supervision with other management techniques.
- Channel your dog's energy into other pursuits.
- Discourage your digger with barriers and/or repellents. If your Brittany has a favorite digging spot, fill or cover his hole with a barrier he can't move, at least temporarily to break his habit. If he digs under the fence, sink a few inches (cm) of chicken wire or chain link fencing along the fence line. If he digs into the soft garden soil, bury chicken wire under a layer of soil to block him.

- You might try various products that are meant to discourage digging, but don't rely on them alone. For one thing, they don't provide any alternative outlet for the urge to "do something" that started your dog digging in the first place. Secondly, in my experience a lot of them (such as cayenne pepper and various commercial formulations) don't work very well and smell bad. In addition, a few (moth balls, for instance) are highly toxic and just not good for you or your dog.

If your dog is determined to dig, consider giving him a legal spot where he can indulge himself. Pick a spot with loose sand or sandy soil, or build your dog a sandbox. Put up a barrier to control flying sand or dirt, and make sure that the sand is deep enough to let your dog really dig in. To encourage him to dig in that spot, hide a treat or a toy in it a few inches (cm) down. Then encourage your dog to dig up the prize. Repeat several times over a few days, and supervise your dog whenever he's outdoors. If you see him digging anywhere else, calmly and quietly take him to his digging spot and encourage him to dig there.

Try giving your dog his own area in which to dig.

WHEN TO SEEK PROFESSIONAL HELP

If your Brittany has a problem behavior that you can't fix on your own, don't let it continue. Get professional help from your veterinarian and/or a qualified professional trainer or behaviorist. The longer an unwanted behavior continues, the harder it is to stop, so for your sake and that of your dog, get the help you both need asap.

Be aware, too, that certain gardening products meant to enhance soil may be like olfactory "Dig Here" signs to your dog. Fish emulsion, bonemeal, and blood meal, for example, are made from animal parts and they smell like it to your dog, even if the odor is negligible to your feeble human nose. Your dog may dig to find the rest of the body.

House Soiling

Most Brittanys are reasonably easy to housetrain (see Chapter 6) if they are given a chance. Puppies, of course, need help because they don't yet have full control of their bodies. Dogs with certain health issues may be unable to control their bodily functions, and elderly dogs sometimes become fully or partially incontinent. Sexually intact (unspayed or unneutered) dogs who are not properly trained may mark territory indoors as well as out with urine. Some older dogs have learned to ignore filth by being forced to live in it. Sometimes, though, a healthy adult soils the house

simply because his house training was never complete.

How to Manage It

Whatever the underlying cause, if your dog is prone to soiling the house, you need to manage the problem while you train or retrain him. Review "Housetraining" in Chapter 6, and stick to a regular training routine for as long as it takes. If he is not completely reliable, don't give him the run of the house, and don't let him be loose even in one room when you cannot supervise him. Don't expect your dog to be housetrained according to some arbitrary schedule. He may be trained in ten days or it may take ten months. Help your dog get it right.

If your dog was housetrained and then began to soil the house, or if training seems to take longer than you think it should, speak to your vet. Some medical problems, including diseases, infections, parasites, hormone changes, and other factors, can make it difficult or impossible for your dog to control his bladder or bowels, and treatment may solve the problem.

Jumping Up

A dog who jumps on people uninvited is a nuisance and a hazard. It may be cute when a roly-poly puppy jumps up and whines for attention, but it isn't so cute once he's no longer a puppy. Unfortunately, by that time he may have learned that people pay attention when he jumps up. You may think the message is clearly "Get off me" when you holler

A dog who jumps on people is a nuisance and a hazard.

and wave your arms at your joyfully leaping dog, but he probably sees it all as a great game.

How to Manage It

As with other behaviors, the best "fix" is prevention from the start—never pet or pick up your puppy unless he has all four feet on the ground.

What if your Brittany is no longer a baby? Don't despair—you can stop his jumping up. Please don't use violent methods, though—a knee to the chest or stepping on his back toes can seriously injure your dog and doesn't work all that well anyway. Here are some methods that do work if you are consistent.

- **Ignore your dog when he jumps up.** Fold your arms over your chest, look up, turn your back, and ignore your dog until he has four on the floor. Behavior that is not rewarded disappears. To make this method work, though, you need to plan ahead. Wear old clothes around your dog, and give yourself time to allow him to quit jumping up. If he's come to expect a more active reaction from you, it may take him a while to catch on, but once he knows that you become extremely boring when he jumps up, he will quit. Be sure to reward him when he stays down—a treat occasionally, and frequent praise and petting.

- **Direct your dog to do something else, like sit or lie down.** Ideally, you will anticipate his jumping up and give him the alternative command before he jumps. If you're a little slow with the command, though, you can still use this method—just tell him what to do and reward him when he does it. Soon he will anticipate the command and sit or lie down for his reward rather than jump on you.

One of the biggest problems with jumping dogs is that they jump on other people, and people are much harder to retrain than are dogs! To teach your dog not to jump on other people, put a leash on him when you expect to encounter someone so that you have control of your dog. When greeting someone, ask the person not to touch or talk to your dog until he does what you told him (such as sit). Only when he does what you want should the person pet him or even give him a treat. Until your Brittany has learned never to jump on people, you will need to manage his encounters so that other people don't sabotage your training efforts.

Nipping

Brittanys are generally not aggressive, but puppies and adolescents often mouth and even nip a bit. Most dogs outgrow the behavior as they mature. But why does your puppy have to nip and mouth everyone in the first place?

For one thing, he uses his mouth (along with his nose) to explore the world. This is not really so different from human toddlers who stick everything in their mouths. A more important reason is that puppies use their mouths to interact socially with other dogs.

How to Manage It

Your pup has to learn that people don't appreciate being nipped, slobbered on, chomped on, or mouthed, not even in play. Here are simple effective ways to teach him:

- **Replace the attractive body part with something he is allowed to chew.** When he takes your finger or ankle in his mouth, gently offer him a chew toy, and pet him and praise him for doing something good. He'll learn that hands are gentle things for belly and ear rubs, not organic chew toys.
- **When your pup chomps on you, say "Ouch!"** Then stand up, cross your arms so your hands are out of reach, and ignore him. If he jumps up, continue to ignore him—maybe he will learn two lessons at once! Your hands are out of reach, so he may go for your ankles or your pants. If he is in a safe place, leave him briefly (no more than a minute), then calmly return and play gently, encouraging him again to play with you but chew on the chew toy.

PROBLEM BEHAVIOR CHECKLIST

- ✓ Preventing unwanted behavior is much easier than fixing it once it's a habit.
- ✓ Basic obedience training and plenty of exercise prevent or fix a lot of problem behaviors.
- ✓ To put an end to excessive barking, first figure out why your dog is so noisy.
- ✓ Provide safe chew toys and manage your dog to prevent dangerous and destructive chewing.

- ✓ Digging can be stopped or redirected through training, exercise, and redirection.
- ✓ House soiling is often a result of incomplete housetraining or a symptom of a medical issue.
- ✓ Jumping up and nipping are annoying and potentially dangerous behaviors that can be prevented nonviolently with consistent, positive training methods.

- **If your little nipper is really determined, try Plan C:** Make yourself taste icky. Pet supply stores sell spray-on products that taste terrible; most have names with "bitter" in them. Menthol vapor rubs also discourage chewing and licking, but if you use one on your hands, be sure to wash them well before you handle food or rub your own or your dog's eyes. I would also wear old clothes or test a discreet spot to be sure that the product doesn't stain. Use the "bad taste" approach in conjunction with other training so that your dog learns not just to avoid the nasty stuff but also to refrain from mouthing you.

- **Let your puppy or adolescent rest.** Sometimes puppies and young dogs just get so tired they can't think straight. Like human children, tired puppies sometimes get cranky or overreactive because they need to sleep. If your pup has been playing for quite a while and acts a bit wild and crazy, take him out for a potty break, then put him into his crate with a small treat and a chew toy and let him rest.

  Never slap or hit your puppy or dog for mouthing (or anything else). Hitting will not teach the lesson you intend. If your puppy is bold and confident, he may think that you're playing and nip even more. If he thinks that you're trying to hurt him (which you are), he may bite

A well-behaved Brittany is a pleasure to own.

for real, which is very different from play nipping, and potentially a serious problem for both of you. A less bold puppy or dog may develop other problem behaviors as a result of rough handling—submissive urination, hand shyness (cowering when hands are coming toward him), and general fearfulness. He may even try to defend himself and become a fear biter out of desperation.

If you believe that your dog has gone beyond nipping to actual aggressive behavior, get professional help. Don't delay—such behavior will not fix itself and if not addressed effectively, it can be dangerous. Consult your veterinarian first to be sure that your dog isn't reacting to a health issue. Then find an experienced positive-reinforcement trainer or behaviorist who has worked successfully with aggressive dogs. Ask your vet or obedience instructor for referrals, or visit the Association of Pet Dog Trainers' website at www.apdt.com for a list of positive trainers in your area.

Chapter
8

Activities With
Your Brittany

One of the best things about having a dog in your life is all the ways you can have fun together. This is especially true with an active dog like a Brittany, so let's take a quick look at activities that you and your dog can share for the good of you both.

Traveling With Your Dog—or Not

What's more fun than going places and doing things with your dog? Not much! And although a well-behaved healthy Brittany is a fairly undemanding traveling companion, you can do a few things to make traveling with your Brittany easier and safer.

Remember that your behavior as a dog owner affects all of us. Many public places no longer allow dogs, the reason being that their people behaved badly. Whether in your own neighborhood or during travel, especially during hotel and motel stays, be courteous. Don't leave your dog alone to bark or cause problems, and don't leave messes of any kind for someone else to clean.

Travel by Car

Many people let their dogs ride loose in their vehicles, but that's a practice you may want to reconsider. If you have to hit the brakes, your unrestrained dog can be thrown forward, possibly injuring himself or someone else. If your Brittany gets excited about something, he may interfere with the driver, or again, hurt someone. Your dog and the people around him will be much safer if he's riding in a secure crate that will not only restrain him but also protect him in case of collision. Another option is a properly fitted doggy seat belt. It won't protect your dog as well as a crate can, but it will keep him from being thrown around or let loose. In any case, your Brittany should ride in the back seat—a deploying air bag can injure or even kill a dog.

Your dog should never be left alone in a parked car, regardless of the weather.

Ask the Expert

BRITTANYS AND HEATSTROKE

Q: How can I tell whether my Brittany is suffering from heatstroke?

A: "Signs of heatstroke in dogs can include labored breathing, elevated body temperature (often greater than 105°F [40.5°C]), and collapse. Vomiting and diarrhea can also occur, and the dog's gums may appear bright red," says Lisa A. Notestine, DVM, MT (ASCP). "Heatstroke is a life-threatening emergency and requires immediate treatment to cool your dog. Suggestions for immediate cooling include wrapping cool wet towels around the dog's neck (applying fresh towels every few minutes) and running water over the dog's body, especially his abdomen and between the rear legs. It is important not to overcool the dog. It is also important that you take your dog to a veterinarian as soon as possible, preferably while you are trying to cool him, as the dog may require further medical treatment." Dr. Notestine suggests the following sites as sources of accurate information about first aid and other veterinary issues: the American Veterinary Medical Association (AVMA) website (www.avma.org), the American Animal Hospital Association (AAHA) website (www.healthypet.com), and VeterinaryPartner.com (www.veterinarypartner.com).

Before you take your Brittany along in the car, be sure that he won't have to stay there when you park in warm weather. The temperature in a parked vehicle can become deadly for your dog in just a few minutes, even with the windows cracked, so if your dog won't be able to get out of the car when you do, leave him safe at home.

Travel by Air

Flying somewhere that you want to take your dog? Be aware that unless your Brittany is a puppy still small enough to ride in an approved carrier that will fit under the seat, he will have to travel as cargo in an airline-approved carrier with food and water containers. Your dog will need a health certificate issued by a veterinarian within ten days prior to the flight. Be aware, too, that in extreme weather live animals are not accepted as cargo.

Most airlines limit the number of animals allowed on a flight, so make your reservations in plenty of time. Whether he rides in the cabin or in cargo, your Brittany should wear identification, and you should carry a leash with you. Different carriers have

If you choose to board your dog, visit the kennel ahead of time.

board your dog at a boarding kennel or hire a pet sitter to come to your home. In either case, ask for references and check them—knowing that other dog lovers have been happy with the care their pets received will help you worry a lot less while you're traveling.

Some pet sitters visit several times each day to take your dog out, feed him, and play with him. Others stay in your home during your absence. If you need to find a sitter, ask your veterinarian or groomer for recommendations. Have the prospective sitter visit your home to be sure that she's comfortable with your Brittany and vice versa, and be sure that you know what she is and is not willing to do with and for your dog. Ideally, the sitter you hire will be a member of one of the national pet sitters' organizations. Find out whether she's had canine first-aid training and whether she's prepared to handle emergency procedures. Does she have a reliable vehicle? After getting all of this information, follow your instincts. Your Brittany will be happier and safer at home only if he gets gentle, reliable care.

different policies and not all airlines transport animals, so check with the airline you are using well in advance for booking requirements, prices, restrictions, and so on.

Pet Sitting and Boarding Options

You may have to travel sometimes without your Brittany, and you'll have to arrange for someone to care for him. If you have a friend or family member who is capable and willing, that may be your best option. If not, you will need to

If you choose to board your dog, visit the kennel ahead of time. It should be clean and free of hazards that could injure your dog. The kennel area should be fenced so that if your dog slips out of his run, he'll still be confined. Someone should be on site at all times, and plans should be in place to handle emergencies and to prevent theft or vandalism. Be sure that you understand what the basic fees include and how much any extra services will cost. Naturally you want to be confident that dogs in the facility are healthy, but if you prefer not to vaccinate your dog every year, or to omit certain vaccinations (see Chapter 9), boarding may not be an option for your dog.

Sports and Activities

Brittanys particpate in many activities, both competitive and noncompetitive. This section will give you an idea of some of the things many Brittanys and their owners enjoy doing.

Like all other active dogs, Brittanys enjoy doing all of the things that people enjoy doing with dogs—taking long walks, playing fetch the ball or flying disc, hiking, backpacking, camping, and just hanging out together. Truth to tell, those are some of the best things you can do with your dog!

You may also want to participate in some activities that require more advanced training. Many experienced Brittany breeders, rescuers, and owners are happy to help newcomers get started, so if you want to become active in one of more of these activities with your dog, contact your local Brittany club (you can find a listing at http://clubs.akc.org/brit/secretary.htm).

Agility

Brittanys do very well in agility, a sport that requires the handler to direct the dog through a course of jumps, tunnels, and other obstacles in the specified order within a specified time limit. Their energy and built-to-run conformation make them quick and agile, and their natural inclination to follow direction makes them highly responsive to the handler in both training and competition.

Agility trials are sanctioned by several organizations, including the American

Puppy Love

PUPPY SAFETY

It's great fun to watch a puppy play, but be cautious about allowing your Brittany to overtax his youthful body. Developing bones and joints are prone to injuries that can cause lifelong damage, so avoid activities that involve jumping, repetitive twisting motions, or running long distances on hard surfaces until your pup's bones stop growing (usually around 14 to 18 months, but check with your veterinarian to be safe).

To win in Junior Showmanship, the young handler must
demonstrate control and skill in presenting
the dog to the judge, and some knowledge of canine
anatomy, individual breeds, and other dog-related factors.

Kennel Club (AKC), United Kennel Club (UKC), United States Dog Agility Association (USDAA), and others. The obstacles, rules, and titles vary among the organizations, so be sure to read the pertinent rule book before you enter a trial. Ideally, you can take classes with a knowledgeable agility instructor who can keep you and your dog safe from injury as you learn the ropes. You can also "play" agility on simple homemade equipment to have fun with your Brittany and run off some of his energy, but make your dog's safety a high priority when choosing equipment.

Conformation Shows

You've probably seen televised dog shows in which the dogs are trotted around the ring and lined up for judging. Perhaps you've attended some local shows as well. Although the dogs in the ring on any particular day are competing against one another, each dog is also supposed to be judged against the breed standard, which defines the "ideal" dog of that breed. Because dog shows are theoretically designed for evaluating breeding stock, most show-sponsoring organizations limit competition to intact (not spayed or neutered) dogs. To become a champion, a dog must earn points by being judged the best of his or her sex in a particular show.

In the United States, several organizations offer conformation shows and championships. Each is set up a little differently, and the requirements for a championship vary. The AKC conformation program is the best known and largest. Many dog-show enthusiasts also show their dogs in Canadian Kennel Club shows, and occasionally even farther afield.

Junior Showmanship

Many young people aged 10 to 18 enjoy showing their Brittanys in Junior Showmanship, a sport in which the human half of the team is judged instead of the dog. To win in Junior Showmanship, the young handler must demonstrate control and skill in presenting the dog to the judge, and some knowledge of canine anatomy, individual breeds, and other dog-related factors.

Spayed and neutered dogs are allowed in junior showmanship. Your Brittany does not have to be of show quality to team up with a junior handler but should be trained to stack ("stand pretty") and to gait (move at a trot as directed by the judge). And because this is, after all, a show, your junior's dog should always be presented clean, well conditioned, and well groomed.

Hunting, Hunt Tests, and Field Trials

Brittanys were developed to hunt, and many people still use them for hunting. In North America, Brittanys are used primarily to hunt upland game birds, but their French cousins are used for hunting rabbits and other animals as well as birds. A hunting Brittany points, that is, indicates game by freezing in position with his nose pointing toward the hidden prey. The breed is known for having excellent scenting ability, which enables it to find even well-concealed game, and for being very biddable, or willing to do as directed. Brittanys will also retrieve on land and in the water. Many Brittanys are outstanding hunters

SPORTS AND SAFETY

Formal and informal athletic activities are great fun for you and your Brittany, but safety should come first. Here are some tips to prevent injuries and keep play fun for everyone:

- Be sure that your Brittany wears identification. (See Chapter 3.)

- If you walk or jog in poor light, wear light-colored or reflective clothing and put a reflective collar or vest on your Brittany.

- Don't let your Brittany off leash outdoors except in safely fenced areas, and keep him on a leash when he's not inside a fence. One ignored command could get him killed.

- Avoid strenuous activity during hot weather, especially when humidity is high, and offer your dog cool water every 20 to 30 minutes. Keep him in the shade when possible to keep him cooler and to prevent sunburn. Avoid hot surfaces like concrete, blacktop, brick, or tile.

- Never leave your dog in a vehicle in warm weather, even with the windows open.

- Don't run your dog alongside your vehicle—one small error in judgment could get him killed or maimed.

- If you run your dog alongside a bicycle, use a specially designed attachment device for safety.

- Check your Brittany frequently for lumps, bumps, cuts, and other exercise-related injuries.

- Avoid running your dog on hard pavement or gravel that can injure his feet, bones, and joints.

- If your dog shows signs of overexertion (very heavy panting, irregular breathing, stumbling, and reluctance to go on), slow down or stop and rest.

- Don't exercise your dog strenuously right before or right after he eats, and learn to recognize signs of bloat.

- Don't let young children walk your dog without adult supervision. Give older children more freedom on an individual basis, and monitor their dog-walking skills from time to time.

- Teach children never to slide their hands through the loop of a leash or to put a leash around any part of their bodies, particularly their necks. (The same goes for adults!)

- Safety makes playtime more fun for everyone!

when called on to work and outstanding household companions the rest of the time. Their versatility, companionable nature, and manageable size have combined to make them one of the most popular hunting breeds in the United States.

Many Brittany owners with a competitive streak find training for and entering field trials to be rewarding. Field trials are competitive events designed to demonstrate the dog's ability to perform the jobs for which he was bred. The AKC sanctions Pointing Breed Field Trials for breeds designated as pointers, including the Brittany. Classes (called "stakes"') are offered for dogs of all ages at all stages of training, from puppies with little or no training (they are judged on the potential they demonstrate) to "finished" bird dogs who are so well trained and capable that they hunt far from their handlers with little direction. Although the dog is the one being judged in a field trial, the handler also must be skilled at managing and directing the dog. Because dogs running in a field trial can cover great distances, most handlers are on horseback, although handlers may walk if they prefer. Some stakes and field trials are designated walking only. In field trials, the dogs compete against each other to earn various field trial titles, including FC (Field Champion) or, if the handler is not a professional

trainer and handler, AFC (Amateur Field Championship). If an individual dog earns both a show championship (CH) and an FC, that dog is designated a Dual Champion (DC). More than 550 Brittanys have earned this coveted title.

For owners who are interested less in competing than in testing and demonstrating their dogs' pointing and retrieving abilities, the AKC offers Pointing Breed Hunting Tests. In a hunting test, the dog's performance is judged against a standard of perfection— he competes against himself, not against other dogs. Many Brittanys with natural hunting instincts but little training are able to pass the novice level test to earn the title JH (Junior Hunter). The intermediate SH (Senior Hunter) title requires more training and skills, and dogs who pass the MH (Master Hunter) test are reliable, highly skilled hunting dogs who are able to do their job with little guidance from their handler.

Obedience

Formal competition obedience demonstrates the dog's and handler's mastery of various exercises, as well as teamwork between dog and handler. A number of organizations throughout the world, including the AKC and UKC, offer obedience titling programs, and many Brittanys do very well in the sport.

Rally

Rally, or rally obedience, is one of the newest canine sports and one of the most popular. Rally requires the dog and handler to demonstrate specific skills as they negotiate a course of stations, but it is less formal and less rigid than competition obedience or agility, making it a good sport for novice dogs and handlers and for dogs who have limitations that keep them out of the obedience or agility rings.

Many Brittany owners with a competitive streak find training for and entering field trials to be rewarding.

The Association of Pet Dog Trainers (APDT), the AKC, and the UKC all sanction rally trials, and several other organizations are reportedly developing rally programs as well.

Therapy Work

The term "therapy dog" is a sort of catchall term used to refer to a dog who works, usually as a volunteer with his owner, in two different types of settings. Most therapy dogs visit people in any of several types of places, including nursing homes, hospitals, hospices, shelters, schools, and libraries. Therapy dogs have even been brought to disaster sites, including the World Trade Center, to comfort victims and emergency responders. Some therapy dogs work with their owners in more formal therapeutic environments under the direction of a professional therapist, teacher, or doctor.

Canine-assisted therapy can be very rewarding, but it's not all fun and games. If you think that you would like to become involved in therapy work with your Brittany, consider the following questions carefully:

- Do you like to volunteer?
- Can you commit to a regular schedule?
- Is your dog obedient and well behaved around new people and in unusual environments?
- Do you and your Brittany both enjoy meeting all kinds of people?

Check It Out

TRAVEL CHECKLIST

You should be able to answer "yes" to all of these questions before you venture into canine-assisted therapy.

Some institutions will let you to bring your dog for visits with few questions asked, but there are advantages to having your Brittany certified as a therapy dog before you visit. Certification is based on an evaluation process that verifies that your dog has the temperament and behavior necessary for therapy work. In addition, most therapy organizations provide insurance coverage for their members while they are visiting in a therapy context. Many hospitals, nursing homes, libraries, and other institutions, as well as training and kennel clubs, have therapy programs, or you may be able to arrange individual visits with a particular institution.

Tracking

Tracking is a sport that comes naturally to most dogs, and their superb scenting abilities make Brittanys natural tracking dogs. The whole point of tracking is for the dog to follow a trail of human scent, which he already knows how to do. Your only job is to help him understand which human you want him to track.

Informal tracking doesn't have to be time consuming, but if you want your Brittany to earn a tracking title, be prepared to invest several hours a week in training and practice. Not only does your dog need to understand his job, but you need to learn to read your dog and to trust him on the track. In addition, both you and your dog must be fit enough to walk long distances over rough terrain. Tracking clubs exist in some areas, and many obedience clubs have tracking groups that train together. The AKC and ASCA both offer tracking titles, as do other organizations throughout the world.

Chapter 9

Health of
Your Brittany

Your Brittany will live a longer, healthier life if you take steps to protect him from the dangers and diseases that can threaten his well-being. You are his first line of defense, the one who will provide for his immediate needs and take him to the veterinarian when necessary for professional care. Let's see what you can do to promote your Brittany's health from puppyhood through his senior years.

Finding the Right Veterinarian

One of the most important people in your Brittany's life is his veterinarian. His vet will protect him from disease and parasites and give you information and tools you need to keep him healthy and sound. You should feel confident not only about your veterinarian's medical knowledge and skills but also about his or her willingness to answer your questions and respond to your concerns. If you have had a pet before, you may already have a veterinarian you like. If not, here are some suggestions to help you choose the best vet for your needs and your dog's long-term health.

Ask your breeder, friends, and family who they see for their pets' care, and use their recommendations as a starting point. If possible, visit the facility and interview any likely candidates before your dog needs care. Most vets will talk to you for a few minutes at no charge, but even if you have to pay for an office visit, it's worth it to know that your Brittany's health—in fact, his life—will be in good hands.

You needn't want to socialize with your vet, but you should feel comfortable discussing your dog's care. The vet should listen to your concerns and answer your questions. The atmosphere of the practice in which the vet works is also important, because you will interact with veterinary technicians, assistants, and receptionists and with

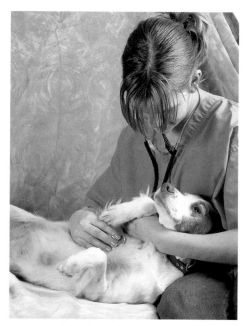

You should feel comfortable discussing your dog's care with your vet.

the other vets when your regular vet is unavailable. You should feel confident and comfortable with the personnel, and you and your dog should be treated with respect.

People are the most important asset of a veterinary practice, but you may also want to consider some or all of the following factors when choosing:

- Are the office hours convenient?
- How do they handle emergency care?
- Can you choose the vet you will see? What if your regular vet is not available?
- Are appointments available on short notice if your dog is ill or injured?
- Do they follow up-to-date vaccination protocols, and are they willing to address your vaccination concerns?
- Do they offer or support alternative approaches to prevention and disease?
- What are their payment and billing policies?
- Do they offer any discounts (such as for multiple pets or seniors)?
- Can you drop your dog off and pick him up later if necessary? Will you be charged a boarding fee? Will you be able to see the vet when you pick your dog up?
- Do they offer other services, such as boarding, training, or grooming?
- Are the waiting room, exam rooms, holding or boarding kennels, and operating area clean and in good repair?

Routine Veterinary Care

Routine regular examinations, vaccines, and preventive medications are essential for your dog's health and well-being. You may be tempted to skip routine vet visits to save money if your Brittany appears to be in good health, but neglecting routine checkups could cost you more in the long run and lead to serious, even life-threatening, health problems for your dog.

As long as your adult Brittany is in good health and is protected against parasites, he probably needs to see the vet only once a year for a checkup and, when appropriate, for vaccinations. Puppies, elderly dogs, and dogs with chronic health problems should see their vets more often.

During a routine examination, your vet will check your Brittany's:

- teeth and gums for tartar, swelling, or inflammation
- ears for infection, injury, or other problems
- eyes for appearance and pupil response
- skin and coat for parasites, bumps, lesions, and other problems
- weight, temperature, respiration, and heart rate

Your vet will probably draw blood to

Ask the Expert

Q: What is the best age to have my Brittany spayed or neutered?

A: "Traditionally, it has been recommended that you have your dog spayed/neutered at around six months of age," says veterinarian Lisa A. Notestine, DVM, MT (ASCP). "Contrary to popular belief, there is no benefit to letting your female dog go through a heat cycle before she is spayed; rather, it has been shown that spaying before she goes into heat reduces her risk of developing mammary cancer. Also, neutering a male dog before sexual maturity helps to prevent many unwanted behaviors associated with testosterone production." Notestine concludes that, "Ultimately the best time to spay/neuter your dog is a decision made between you and your veterinarian, but around six months of age would be considered appropriate."

screen for signs of disease, including heartworm, and possibly to perform a titer test for immunity to disease, and will need a fecal specimen to check for intestinal parasites. If your Brittany is due for vaccinations, your vet will give them after the exam. The vet will also prescribe other medications as needed and, depending on the results of the examination, may recommend additional tests.

Vaccinations

Dogs are susceptible to a number of infectious diseases. Some are relatively mild, but others can kill your dog or leave him with lifelong problems. Fortunately, vaccinations are available to prevent or limit the severity of many common canine diseases.

Most canine vaccines are injected subcutaneously (under the skin) or intramuscularly (into the muscle). A few are administered by nasal sprays. Vaccines are usually given to dogs in combination shots that protect against more than one disease and are classified in two ways. Core vaccinations are considered essential protection against the most common canine diseases: distemper, parvovirus, canine infectious hepatitis, and parainfluenza. Rabies vaccine is also a core vaccine and is required by law in some areas. Noncore vaccinations provide protection against diseases for which a particular dog may or may not be at risk.

All dogs should receive the core vaccinations. Your veterinarian may also recommend some of the noncore vaccinations, depending on your dog's age, general health, potential for exposure to the disease, and vaccination history, including any adverse reactions he has had to vaccines in the past.

Changing Approaches to Vaccination

Many veterinarians and pet owners have become increasingly concerned about health and behavior problems associated with overvaccination. As a result, the American Veterinary Medical Association (AVMA), most veterinary colleges, and many veterinarians and dog owners have shifted away from comprehensive annual vaccinations. Although a single alternative approach has yet to emerge, there is general agreement that puppies and adult dogs who have not previously been vaccinated need at least the core vaccines to stimulate their immune systems. Some people believe that this initial sequence of vaccinations provides lifelong protection. Others believe that boosters are still needed but not every year.

Some use titers to check immunity and revaccinate only when immunity is low. Rabies vaccination is the exception and is required by law in many places. (See "Rabies."). It's important to remember that, used properly, vaccines offer your Brittany the best available protection against infectious diseases. Work with your veterinarian to decide which vaccines to give and on what schedule.

Diseases to Be Vaccinated Against

Here, in alphabetical order, are the most common diseases against which your Brittany may be vaccinated.

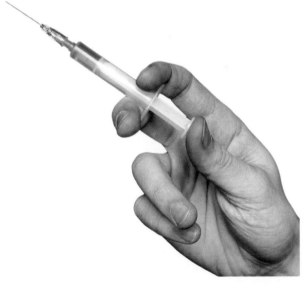

Most canine vaccines are injected subcutaneously (under the skin) or intramuscularly (into the muscle).

...ella (Kennel Cough)

Bordetellosis, often called just plain bordetella (after *Bordetella,* the name of the genus of bacteria that are its causative organism), is a disease of the respiratory tract. It causes a horrible-sounding cough and is sometimes accompanied by copious nasal discharge, but bordetella usually isn't very serious in an otherwise healthy adult dog. For a young puppy or elderly dog or one with other health issues, bordetella can be deadly. Bordetella vaccines are usually given in a nasal spray. Although most boarding kennels and certain other canine businesses require client dogs be vaccinated against bordetella, some vets and owners believe that their dogs' own immune systems protect them better against more strains of the disease than do vaccinations.

Coronavirus

Coronavirus is a viral disease that attacks the lining of the small intestine. The signs include depression, loss of appetite, and lethargy, progressing to vomiting (sometimes with blood in the vomit) and projectile diarrhea that is yellowish and often contains blood and mucus.

Coronavirus occurs only in certain geographical areas, so many veterinarians do not recommend vaccination for dogs who are not at risk.

Distemper

Canine distemper is caused by a widespread and highly contagious virus that attacks the nervous system and causes respiratory problems, vomiting, and diarrhea. Most puppies and about half of adult dogs who contract the disease die from it. Survivors often lose some or all of their vision, hearing, and sense of smell and may be partially or completely paralyzed. The canine distemper vaccine is a core vaccine. Puppies receive three or four vaccinations against distemper, and many vets recommend vaccination for adults, especially older dogs.

Hepatitis

Canine infectious hepatitis is caused by a highly contagious virus that is shed in the urine of infected dogs. It attacks many tissues but usually does the most damage to the liver.

The hepatitis vaccine is a critical core vaccine. Puppies are normally given a series of three shots; adult dogs may be revaccinated annually or less frequently.

Leptospirosis

Leptospirosis, or "lepto," is a deadly disease caused by bacteria that attack the kidneys and spread easily in the urine of infected animals. Lepto causes vomiting, convulsions, vision problems, and eventual kidney failure. Several different strains of the disease occur, but it is rare in most places.

Unfortunately, vaccination is not very effective against the most common strain of the disease, and serious reactions to the vaccine are not uncommon. Many veterinarians and owners choose not to vaccinate against lepto when the risk of exposure is low. If you believe that your Brittany is at risk, consider having the leptospirosis vaccine given by itself, and stay at the clinic for half an hour or so after the shot is given in case your dog has an adverse negative reaction. If he does, do not revaccinate for lepto, and be sure that this information is included in your dog's veterinary records.

Lyme Disease

Lyme disease, or Lyme's, is a bacterial disease that causes generalized illness in animals and humans. It is transmitted by ticks, particularly tiny deer ticks, that feed on the blood of infected people or animals and then transmit the bacteria to subsequent hosts through bites. In the United States, Lyme disease is found primarily in Atlantic and Pacific coast states and in parts of the Midwest. You cannot catch Lyme's directly from your dog.

Lyme disease in dogs is usually diagnosed when the disease causes lameness, pain, and sometimes swelling in one or more joints. Other signs of the disease may include fever, lack of appetite, dehydration, lethargy, and swollen lymph nodes. Caught early, Lyme disease can usually be cured with antibiotics. Undetected, or left untreated, Lyme disease causes crippling arthritis and may damage the kidneys.

Most vets do not recommend routine vaccination for Lyme disease when risk of exposure is low. Talk to your vet about current recommendations for your area and your Brittany's level of risk. If you and your dog frequent areas where ticks

Most vets do not recommend routine vaccination for Lyme disease when risk of exposure is low.

are active, ask about tick preventives, and check both your dog and yourself thoroughly after every outing. (See also "Ticks.")

Parainfluenza

Parainfluenza is a viral infection of the respiratory tract that causes symptoms similar to flu in people. One of the core vaccines, parainfluenza vaccine is usually given to puppies in a series of three vaccinations, often in combination with other vaccines.

Parvovirus

Parvovirus, or "parvo," is caused by a highly contagious virus that attacks the intestinal tract, heart muscle, and white blood cells. Most puppies and many dogs die within two or three days of showing initial signs of the disease, even when given intensive veterinary care. Signs of parvo include severe, foul-smelling diarrhea, vomiting, high fever, loss of appetite, and depression. Parvovirus is shed in the feces of infected dogs and is easily transported on shoes, paws, and clothing. The virus is long lived and impervious to most disinfectants and to extreme temperatures, making it very hard to eliminate once it enters an area. Parvo is especially deadly to puppies, and survivors often suffer heart problems throughout their lives. This is a critical core vaccine. Puppies are given a series of three parvo vaccinations, and boosters are recommended on varying schedules for adults, especially seniors.

Rabies

Rabies is a viral disease that attacks the central nervous system of any mammal, including people. Rabies, which is endemic in many parts of the world, is spread through the saliva of infected animals, usually by way of a bite, although it can also enter the body from a lick to an open wound or mucous membrane. Prevention is crucial because once symptoms appear, rabies is always fatal. That is why laws in the United States, Canada, and some other countries require that pets be vaccinated against rabies. Those countries that are free of rabies want to remain that way, so they quarantine incoming animals.

Rabies takes two forms. Furious rabies causes the victim to foam at the mouth and behave aggressively. Animals affected with the dumb form of the disease may not display obvious signs of infection; eventually, though, they will become paralyzed, usually starting with the lower jaw and spreading through the limbs and vital organs until the animal dies. If you think that you or your dog have been exposed to rabies, seek medical attention immediately.

Rabies is a critical core vaccine. Puppies should be vaccinated against rabies at three to four months of age and then given booster shots according to the laws where you live.

Parasites

Your Brittany, like many other animals, is a potential host for a variety of parasites, which are organisms that take their nutrition from other living creatures. Fortunately, you can keep your dog and your home free of these creepy critters through good preventive care and by responding quickly if you see or suspect that your dog has picked up any unwanted passengers.

Internal Parasites

Many types of parasites can occupy the digestive systems of dogs and other animals. Some parasites cause no serious problems, but many cause diarrhea, bloody stools, weight loss, dry coat, and/or vomiting. Some parasites can even lie dormant in your dog's body

Many parasites are spread by intermediate hosts, such as mosquitoes.

PUPPY VACCINATIONS

Puppies need to be vaccinated to enable their immune systems to fend off deadly diseases. Work with your vet to set up a puppy vaccination schedule. At the same time, have your pup checked for parasites and treated as necessary, and use preventive medications as recommended by your veterinarian. Finally, unless your pup is an outstanding representative of the breed, have him neutered or her spayed.

in egg or larval stages only to become activated when their host is under stress, or in the case of roundworms in a pregnant bitch, until they can infest prenatal puppies.

Although some intestinal parasites are visible to the naked eye, many can be detected only with a microscope. Once they are identified, some parasites are fairly easy to eliminate with the right medication. Others are tougher to kill, and you may have to treat your dog more than once to eliminate them. Most pet dogs should have a fecal specimen checked annually, usually as part of their regular checkups. If your Brittany spends a lot of time in areas frequented by other animals, wild or domestic, two or three checks a year would be better.

You may occasionally see worms in your dog's stool, especially if you have a young puppy. Don't panic—worms are disgusting but they are not a medical emergency. Collect a specimen and take it to your vet so that the vet can identify the parasite and prescribe the right medication to eliminate it. Most over-the-counter dewormers and home remedies are less effective than those your vet can prescribe, and some are dangerous, especially when combined with certain other products, so don't waste money and time or risk your dog's health. Your vet can also tell you how to prevent parasites from spreading to your other pets.

Some parasites will happily inhabit people, so until your dog is declared worm-free by your vet, be sure to wash your hands with soap and hot water after handling him and after performing "poop patrol." Teach your children to do the same. In addition, be sure to remove dog feces from your back yard several times a week (daily if you have more than one dog), pick up after your dog in public places, and avoid walking your Brittany where other dog owners don't pick up after their dogs.

Now let's have a look at the most common internal parasites that attack dogs.

Coccidia

Coccidia are protozoans (single-celled organisms) that attack the small intestine. In a healthy adult dog, coccidia may cause no outward symptoms. In a young, unhealthy, or stressed animal, however, they can cause coccidiosis, characterized by intestinal cramping, bloody diarrhea, dehydration, anemia, and/or weight loss. Stress may trigger an outbreak of coccidiosis in a dog who has been infected but is asymptomatic. Coccidiosis is usually treated with drugs that prevent the protozoans from reproducing. This gives the dog's immune system time to respond and eliminate the coccidia, which usually takes from one to three weeks.

Giardia

Giardiasis, often shortened to giardia, is the name of a disease caused by protozoans of the genus *Giardia,* single-celled parasites that attach themselves to the lining of the small intestine. In a healthy adult Brittany, they may cause no ill effects and go undetected. In a puppy or in an adult whose immune system is impaired, they can cause problems. Giardia can affect people as well as dogs and other animals. Because they are shed in the feces of infected animals, streams and other open water sources are often contaminated with giardia, so try not to let your Brittany drink unpurified water. Signs of giardia include soft, mucus-coated, light-colored stools or extremely foul-smelling diarrhea, as well as weight loss and listlessness. Your vet can diagnose giardia through microscopic examination of a fecal specimen and prescribe appropriate medication.

Heartworms

Heartworms are parasitic worms that infest the heart of a host animal. When

a mosquito bites an infected animal, it ingests heartworm microfilaria (microscopic larvae) present in the animal's blood. When the mosquito bites its next victim, it injects some of the microfilaria into the animal's blood vessels. They travel to the heart, where they mature and reproduce and eventually cause congestive heart failure.

Two types of tests are used to diagnose heartworm infections, both requiring a blood sample. A filter test (or Knott's test) involves examination of blood under a microscope to see whether microfilaria are present. Most veterinarians prefer to use a test that detects heartworm antigens, substances that stimulate the creation of antibodies in the blood, because these tests detect the presence of both adult heartworms and microfilaria. Antigen tests are more expensive than filter tests but more accurate.

Heartworm larvae take about six months to develop into reproducing adults, so a test performed within six months of initial infection will give a false negative result. That's why puppies should be tested at seven months (in case they were infected during their first eight weeks) and adults every year or two. Even if your dog takes preventive medication, he should be tested as recommended. Modern medications are highly effective, but none is 100 percent reliable.

The first sign of heartworm infection is often a soft, deep cough, especially after exercise. Weight loss, weakness, and lethargy are also common, and some infected dogs spit up blood. Signs of heartworm disease don't usually appear until at least a year after initial infection.

Heartworm disease occurs throughout the United States, as well as in other countries. Luckily, preventive medications are highly effective, and

Hookworms can be passed on to nursing puppies through the mom.

as an added bonus, most heartworm preventives control several types of intestinal worms as well. Many vets recommend that dogs be given a heartworm preventive all year round, beginning at eight weeks of age.

If you have an adult Brittany who has not been given a heartworm preventive in the past, have him tested before you begin. Preventive medications can be lethal if given to a dog who is already infected with adult heartworms. If your dog is infected, treatment begins with drug therapy to kill the adult heartworms. During treatment, the patient must be kept quiet to prevent complications or potential death as the worms are killed and flushed out of the heart. Once the adult worms are gone, a follow-up treatment may be given to eliminate any remaining microfilaria.

Your vet can effectively treat worms.

Hookworms

Hookworms are tiny worms that can make your dog very ill. If a bitch has not been kept free of parasites, she may pass hookworms to her puppies in utero or while they are nursing. Chronic hookworm infection scars the lining of the intestine and may cause anemia, diarrhea, weight loss, and weakness. A heavy or long-term infection can be fatal, especially in a puppy who has not had good pre- and post-natal care. Dogs (and people) can also acquire hookworms by walking on soil contaminated with hookworm larvae, which burrow through the skin and enter the bloodstream. Once in the bloodstream, they ride to the small intestine, where they attach themselves with the hooks for which they are named. They suck blood from the tissue, mature, and reproduce. Hookworm infection is diagnosed when microscopic eggs are found in feces. Your vet can prescribe an effective treatment.

Roundworms

Roundworms are extremely common in dogs, especially young puppies.

Even pups who have lived in clean environments and had excellent care sometimes have roundworms. Roundworms look like white strings of spaghetti about 8 inches (20 cm) long. They live in the host animal's intestines and stomach, where they eat food the host has ingested. They are often passed with feces, and a dog with a heavy infection may develop diarrhea and may vomit worms as well. If enough worms are present, an infected puppy may become malnourished and become lethargic; if the infection is allowed to continue, he may stop eating. Roundworms are easy to eliminate, so if you think your Brittany has them, take a fecal sample to your vet for verification and treatment.

Tapeworms

Tapeworms are white worms that are easily identified by their flattened body segments. Tapeworms often reach more than 2 feet (60 cm) in length. They occasionally show up in feces but are more often identified by the tiny rice-like segments that break off from the worm and stick to fur around the animal's anus. Tapeworms cannot be passed directly from dog to dog. They require an intermediate host, such as a flea, rodent, or rabbit, to reproduce and usually find their way to a canine host when the

dog eats the smaller infected critter and ingests tapeworm larvae, which travel to the dog's intestines and develop into adult tapeworms. A long-term tapeworm infection can cause weight loss and other health problems.

General-purpose dewormers do not eliminate tapeworms, so if you see any suspicious rice-like particles around your dog's anus (or, less commonly, lengths of tapeworm in his feces), talk to your vet for proper diagnosis and treatment.

Whipworms

Whipworms are tiny worms that look like bits of thread with one enlarged end. They live in the large intestine, and they may cause colitis and diarrhea, leading to dehydration and other problems if left untreated. Whipworms

Check your dog for fleas and ticks after he's been playing outside.

usually occur in small numbers and can therefore be hard to diagnose. In some cases, several fecal specimens taken over several days must be examined for a definitive diagnosis, although the mucus-like coating commonly found on the stools of infected dogs can help. Once diagnosed, your vet can prescribe effective treatment.

External Parasites

External parasites, including fleas, ticks, and mange mites, live on their host's skin and can make big trouble. Their bites can spread diseases, and the itching of these bites can cause dogs to scratch themselves raw, opening the way for infections and leading to chronic skin irritations and hair loss. Happily, your veterinarian can recommend highly effective products to rid your dog of these nasty pests and keep him parasite-free.

If your Brittany experiences any unexplained hair loss, itching, or skin irritation, take him to your veterinarian for diagnosis and treatment before the problem gets worse. Some parasites will attack people and other animals, so if any human member of your household experiences similar symptoms, see a doctor and tell her about your dog.

NEUTERING

The American Brittany Association (ABA) and Brittany rescue organizations encourage owners to alter (spay or neuter) all but the very best Brittanys in terms of breed type, temperament, and individual and genetic health. Responsible dog ownership includes a commitment to the welfare of any puppies your pet produces, which means that your Brittany should not give birth to or sire a single puppy unless you are willing to care for that puppy throughout his life if necessary. In addition, altering:

- eliminates the risks of pregnancy and whelping, prevents life-threatening cancers or infections of the uterus and ovaries, and reduces the risk of mammary tumors
- eliminates the risk of testicular cancer and reduces the risk of prostate disease
- eliminates most hormone-driven behaviors, such as urine marking
- reduces aggression in both males and females

Altering won't change your Brittany's basic personality, and it won't make your dog fat if you control his or her diet.

Fleas

Fleas are small black or reddish hard-shelled insects that live on the blood of the host animal. They move quickly and can jump many times their own body length, making them very hard to catch. Fleas can drive your dog crazy with itching, and if your Brittany is allergic to flea saliva, even a single bite can cause him to scratch himself raw, opening the way for ongoing skin irritation and open sores. Worse, fleas can carry diseases and tapeworm larvae from one host to the next; in a puppy, a large infestation of fleas can cause anemia.

In some environments, the war against fleas is perpetual because of a favorable climate and other factors. However, if you see parasites on your Brittany or in his environment only occasionally, flea preventives may not be necessary. Talk to your vet and assess your individual situation to make informed choices to control fleas.

If you do find fleas on your dog, or in your home, yard, or vehicle, you need to act quickly to fend off a population explosion. Your vet can recommend relatively safe products to eliminate fleas, eggs, and larvae in your home, yard, and vehicle. As with other drugs and chemicals, follow directions, observe warnings, and avoid products that may harm your dog. Beware of over-the-counter products— some are not very effective, and some are dangerous, especially when combined with one another. Don't bother with flea and tick collars; most are not very effective, and they can cause respiratory distress in some dogs.

Mites

Mites are not insects but microscopic arachnids (relatives of spiders and ticks). Several species of mites live on the skin of dogs, eating skin debris, hair follicles, and tissue and causing various types of mange. Dogs with mange typically develop itchy, flaky, crusty bald spots. They often scratch themselves raw, making it easy for bacteria, viruses, fungi, and other parasites to attack.

Three types of mange mites attack dogs:

Demodex Mites: Demodex mites live in controlled populations on many healthy puppies and dogs without causing problems. Some puppies, though, are less resistant; as a result, the mites reproduce more rapidly than normal and cause a condition called demodectic mange, or demodex. Seen most often in puppies from three months to a year old, demodex typically causes thinning of the hair around the eyes, mouth, and front legs. Demodex usually runs its course within two or three months without causing major problems, but some puppies develop oozing sores and crusty skin and lose hair over large areas, so if you suspect a problem, see your vet as soon as possible. In adult dogs, demodex usually develops only when the immune system is compromised by other factors. Poor nutrition or stress can lead to adult-onset demodex, which is why this type of mange is not uncommon in shelter and rescue dogs. To control demodectic mange in adults, the underlying cause must be resolved so that the immune system can do its job.

Sarcoptic Mites: Sarcoptic mange (scabies) is caused by mites that burrow under their victim's skin to lay eggs,

Ticks are small arachnids that carry a number of diseases.

If your dog appears unusually lethargic or displays any major changes in appetite, contact your vet.

from which larvae quickly emerge, develop into adult mites, and lay more eggs. Scabies causes intense itching, oozing sores, crusty ear tips, secondary infections, and hair loss on the ears, elbows, legs, and face and, in advanced cases, the dog's entire body. Quick veterinary response is critical not only for the dog's sake but also to prevent the mites from spreading to the human family. Because the burrowing mites often don't show up in skin scrapings, some veterinarians prefer to treat for scabies based on symptoms even if no mites are found.

Cheyletiellosis: Cheyletiellosis, or "walking dandruff," is caused by tiny white mites that look like dandruff moving around on the dog's head, neck, and back. Although the *Cheyletiella* mites cause mild itching in puppies and are easily passed from one dog to another and to people, cheyletiellosis is easily cured with proper diagnosis and treatment.

Ringworm
Ringworm is not a worm at all but a highly contagious fungal infection. It typically appears first as a sore-looking bald ring on the skin, spreading quickly and easily

from one pet to another and to people.

Ringworm, like all other fungal infections, is very difficult to treat. Don't waste time or money on over-the-counter or home remedies; they will probably be ineffective and will give the infection time to become better established, making subsequent treatment even more difficult. Your veterinarian can prescribe effective drugs and tell you how to prevent the infection from spreading.

Ticks

Ticks are small arachnids (relatives of spiders and mites). Like fleas, ticks eat blood. They also carry a number of diseases, including babesiosis, anaplasmosis, ehrlichiosis, East Coast fever, relapsing fever, Rocky Mountain spotted fever, and Lyme disease. Ticks are common in fields and woods and may be carried into your yard and home by animals and people.

Unfed ticks are round and flat, rather like a brown lentil. They have eight legs and a tiny little head. After a meal, a tick will swell up and look like a bean with legs. Deer ticks are so small that they are almost impossible to find until after they've eaten.

If you live or travel where ticks are likely to hang out, check your dog frequently. Pay special attention to places like the ears, armpits, and the groin area, where ticks can easily hide. If you find a tick that has not yet fastened onto your dog's flesh, pick it up with a tissue and either flush it down the toilet or seal it into a plastic bag and put it in the garbage. If the tick has already attached itself, follow these steps to remove it safely:

- Dab the tick with a cotton ball soaked in alcohol, iodine, or a strong saline solution—this will make it loosen its grip.
- Grasp the tick's body firmly with a tick remover or tweezers and pull it straight out. Don't twist or squeeze—you may leave the head behind or force disease-filled fluid into the victim.
- If you remove a very small tick, show it to your veterinarian for identification. Tiny deer ticks carry Lyme disease, which affects people as well as dogs.
- Unless you pulled its head off, the tick is still alive, so handle it carefully. Drop it into alcohol, flush it down the toilet, or seal it into a plastic bag for disposal.
- Clean the area with alcohol or antibacterial cleanser, dry it, and apply antibacterial ointment. Wash your hands and tools with antibacterial soap.
- Keep an eye on the area for a few days, and call your vet if it becomes inflamed or develops a rash.

If you find a lot of ticks on your dog or find them frequently, ask your vet about safe products to repel and kill ticks during warm weather.

Genetic Disorders in Brittanys

As a breed, Brittanys are generally healthy dogs, but some genetic problems do exist. This does not mean that your dog will have any of these disorders, but it does mean that you should be aware of their presence in the

FIRST-AID KIT

Most people who own active dogs occasionally have use for a first-aid kit. You can purchase a ready-made pet first-aid kit, but it's easy and less costly to put one together yourself. Here's what you need:

- 3% hydrogen peroxide (write the purchase date on the label, and discard and replace the bottle once a year)
- a broad-spectrum antibiotic cream
- a medicine syringe for administering liquids
- a muzzle that fits your dog
- a small bottle of mild liquid dish detergent to remove contaminants from coat and skin (Dawn is commonly used)
- a small rectal thermometer and a sterile lubricant (*not* petroleum jelly)
- a veterinary first-aid manual (ask your veterinarian or local Red Cross for recommendations)
- antidiarrheal medication (ask your veterinarian for recommendations)
- directions and telephone numbers for your regular veterinarian and the closest emergency veterinary clinic
- disposable gloves in case you need to handle a contaminated dog
- scissors
- sterile saline eye solution to flush eyes
- the telephone number for the National Animal Poison Control Center (NAPCC): 1-888-4ANI-HELP or 1-900-680-000
- tweezers

Store your supplies in a plastic box with a handle and secure closure. Label it clearly, and keep it where it's easy to find. Take it along if you travel with your dog, or keep a second kit in the car. Once a year, replace all expired medications.

breed. If you plan to purchase a Brittany, use this information to be a smart buyer. Be sure that the parents and grandparents of any puppy you buy have been screened for genetic disorders. In some cases, screening involves tests and certification. In other cases, no tests are available, so you must rely on your breeder's knowledge of the dog's bloodlines. If you plan to adopt a rescued Brittany, the dog's family history will probably not be available, but some of these problems will already be evident in adults. Again, chances are your dog will be healthy!

Now let's look at the most prevalent disorders in the breed.

Hip Dysplasia (HD)

Hip dysplasia (HD) is an inherited condition in which the head of the femur (the long bone of the thigh) does not fit properly into the socket of the pelvis. This poor fit causes excessive wear on the bones of the joint, leading to potentially crippling arthritis. Hip dysplasia affects approximately one in four Brittanys, according to a 1995 health survey conducted. Some affected dogs show signs—soreness and lameness—as early as five or six months of age, but some dysplastic dogs show no clinical signs at all. That's why it's important for breeders to have all Brittanys used for breeding X-rayed and certified free of hip dysplasia by the Orthopedic Foundation for Animals (OFA), the University of Pennsylvania Hip Improvement Program (PennHIP), or the equivalent.

Clinical hip dysplasia—that is, hip dysplasia that results in pain and lameness—is typically treated with any of several surgical procedures, depending on how severe it is. Most dogs recover fully, and, once healed, live normal, active lives.

Seizure Disorders

A small but significant number of Brittanys suffer from inherited seizures, a condition commonly known as epilepsy. A seizure occurs when nerves

As a breed, Brittanys are generally healthy dogs.

in the brain fire without normal controls, causing the animal's muscles to contract repeatedly. Seizures are rarely fatal, but a seizuring dog can injure himself if he falls or bangs into things. In extreme cases, though, seizures may follow one after another so quickly that the dog cannot recover in between, leading to hyperthermia (overheating), hypoglycemia (low blood sugar), exhaustion, permanent brain damage, and possibly death.

The first step toward stopping seizure activity is to identify the cause, if possible. It's important to understand that many factors can cause seizures, including poisons, drugs, head injuries, fever, heatstroke, congenital defects, tumors, diabetes mellitus, hypoglycemia, kidney or liver disease, infectious disease, and others. Some veterinarians are quick to diagnose epilepsy and prescribe treatment based on that diagnosis. If an environmental or underlying medical problem is the cause, such treatment will likely be ineffective in the long term, and failing to identify and treat the real cause can be lethal for your dog. If you have any reservations about the diagnosis, ask your vet to refer you to a veterinary neurologist for a more detailed diagnosis and treatment plan.

If your dog has a seizure, stay calm and stay away from his mouth—he could unintentionally clamp down on you. Touch his body gently and reassure him in a calm voice. Remove or pad sharp or hard objects or furniture, and reduce any nearby stimuli, such as loud music or other sounds or bright or flashing lights. People and pets who cannot be quiet need to leave the area.

If your dog has a seizure, write down the time, the duration, and any triggering factors you notice. Call and let your vet know what has happened. If the seizure lasts more than 15 minutes or if your dog experiences more than one seizure, call your vet or emergency clinic to let them know you're coming, then wrap your dog gently in a sheet or blanket to limit his movements and take him for medical treatment.

If the cause of your dog's seizures can be identified and removed, the seizures will probably stop or be controllable so that your dog can live a reasonably normal life. If the cause cannot be identified, your dog will be diagnosed with idiopathic epilepsy (meaning that the cause is not known). Idiopathic epilepsy is believed to be inherited, and affected dogs usually experience their first seizures when they are between one and five years old. Drug therapy works well for many of these dogs.

Thyroid Disease

Although not as common as in certain other breeds, thyroid disease does occur in some Brittanys. The thyroid gland, which lies in the throat just under the larynx, produces hormones that control growth, development, and the metabolism of proteins, carbohydrates, and fats.

Lack of thyroid hormone causes hypothyroidism, which is often linked to hair loss, obesity or weight gain, lethargy, inflamed ears, abnormally cool skin, or itchy, inflamed, crusty, or scaly skin. It has also been linked to personality problems, including general grumpiness or outright aggression.

Hypothyroidism can be tough to diagnose. The most common test is a simple thyroid (T4) test , but it is not very reliable. A complete blood panel that measures total T4, free T4 (the usable T4 in the blood), TGAA (thyroglobulin autoantibodies), cTSH (canine thyroid stimulating hormone), and sometimes T3 and free T3 is more accurate. If you suspect that your Brittany may be hypothyroid, ask your vet to perform the complete thyroid panel. Thyroid disease can be slow to develop, so if your dog tests negative but still has signs of the disease, have him retested in six to twelve months.

Happily, hypothyroidism can be treated with a relatively inexpensive hormone supplement, usually L-thyroxine, which is generally effective.

Other Illnesses

Not all health issues are inherited, of course. Many are due at least in part to environment and, often, unknown causes, or a combination of many factors. Let's look at a few common ones.

Cancers

Cancers are common in dogs, especially in their later years. Cancer is characterized by the runaway

A sport like agility can keep your Brittany fit and his heart healthy.

Check It Out

HEALTH CHECKLIST

Take the time to find a veterinarian you trust with your Brittany's life.

Keep up with routine health care to maintain your dog's good health.

Work with your vet to set up an appropriate vaccination schedule.

Fend off disease by telling your vet if you see changes in your dog's health or behavior.

Ask your vet about prevention and treatment for parasites.

Maintain high caregiver standards when exploring alternative therapies.

Keep your older Brittany healthy with continuing veterinary care.

---

reproduction of cells that invade nearby body structures; when it spreads to distant parts of the body, a cancer is said to be metastatic. Although young dogs sometimes suffer from cancer, seniors of seven years and older are its more common victims. Some canine cancers have a fairly high cure rate; others are harder to cure or control.

Dogs with cancer are treated much like their human counterparts. The tumor may be surgically removed or reduced in size, especially if the cancer has not spread too far, and chemotherapy drugs or radiation therapy may be used to inhibit or kill the cancer cells. Conventional medical treatments are often supplemented with nutritional and alternative therapies because the dog's overall health can affect his resistance to cancer and chances for recovery. Each dog's prognosis will depend, of course, on the type of cancer, how early it is detected, the dog's age, his health prior to the disease, and other factors.

Older dogs often get noncancerous fatty tumors that usually pose no health threat. Don't panic if your find a lump or growth on your Brittany, but do have your vet look at it. Some canine cancers can be prevented, especially those that involve the reproductive organs. Spayed females have no risk for ovarian or uterine cancer, because they no longer have those organs, and those who are spayed before their first heat have a lower risk of mammary (breast) cancer. Neutered males, similarly, have no risk for testicular cancer. Your own lifestyle affects your dog's health too. For example, there is evidence that dogs who live with smokers are at risk for lung cancer. If you won't quit for yourself, do it for your dog.

Heart Disease

Heart disease is as common in dogs as it is in people, although it behaves a bit differently. Although inherited heart disease is not considered an issue in Brittanys, they can suffer from acquired heart disease due to disease, infection, environmental factors, or aging. Common signs of heart disease in dogs include heavy panting, rapid or irregular breathing, chronic coughing, enlarged abdomen, low stamina, and weight loss. A veterinarian who suspects that your dog has heart disease may suggest diagnostic tests, possibly including electrocardiograms (EKGs), chest X-rays, or sonograms, or refer you to a veterinary cardiologist for specialized care.

You can do a lot to keep your Brittany's heart healthy throughout his life. Most important, don't let him get fat—excess weight puts undue stress on the heart—and see that he gets plenty of exercise as appropriate for his age and overall health and condition. Finally, keep his teeth and gums in good condition (see Chapter 5) because gum disease can contribute to heart disease.

Alternative Therapies

Many people use alternative, complementary, or holistic approaches to canine health care, often in

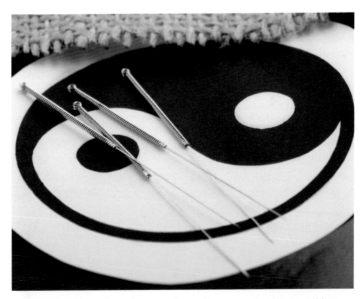

Acupuncture involves the use of needles, massage, heat, and lasers to stimulate the release of hormones, endorphins, and other chemical substances to help the body to fight off pain and disease.

conjunction with more traditional medicine. Alternative approaches vary in philosophy and method, but they are all based on the idea that bodily systems work together to affect physical and emotional health.

Many alternative practitioners are highly qualified, including both veterinarians and lay practitioners. Unfortunately, there are also lots of people handing out bad advice, so be cautious. Inappropriate treatment can delay accurate diagnosis and effective therapies, sometimes with disastrous effects. A licensed veterinarian trained in holistic or alternative techniques combines the best of both worlds. To find a good alternative practitioner, visit the Holistic Veterinary Medical Association (AHVMA) website at www.ahvma.com.

Alternative approaches to canine health care include:

Acupuncture

Acupuncture involves the use of needles, massage, heat, and lasers to stimulate the release of hormones, endorphins, and other chemical substances to help the body to fight off pain and disease.

Chiropractic

Chiropractic is based on the belief that proper alignment of the skeletal system, particularly the spine, is critical to the functioning of the nervous system and overall good health. A practitioner who lacks training in canine anatomy and physiology can cause serious injury, though, so if you want to try chiropractic treatment for your Brittany, find a licensed veterinarian trained in chiropractic.

Herbal Therapy

Herbal therapy is the use of herbs to promote good health and treat disease. Herbal therapy can be highly effective, but some herbs are highly toxic. Use herbal therapies only under the supervision of someone who is very knowledgeable about their properties.

Homeopathy

Homeopathy uses the principle that "like affects like." Homeopathic remedies are generally tiny doses of substances that, in larger doses, would cause symptoms like those of the disease. Be sure that any homeopathic practitioner you consult is qualified to work with dogs; preferably the practitioner will have a degree in veterinary science.

Nutritional Therapy

Nutritional therapy seeks to promote health and treat certain conditions through diet, often by replacing conventional protein sources (such as chicken, beef, and lamb) with alternative sources (such as bison, duck, venison, and others) and by eliminating ingredients thought to be harmful (such as grains, fillers, dyes, and so on).

Your Senior Brittany

The aging process can't be stopped, but its negative effects can often be delayed with good care. Some medical disorders will make your dog age more quickly, but your vet may be able to prevent or treat many of them, which will help lengthen your Brittany's life and improve its quality. Good nutrition, regular exercise, and lots of love and affection will also help make your Brittany's senior years good ones.

Keep your vet informed about changes in your dog's physical health and behavior as he ages. If he becomes seriously ill, discuss your options. Balance the hope offered by expensive or invasive treatments against any extra time it may give your dog, and how much he will enjoy it. Longer is not always better.

With proper nutrition, exercise, and regular vet visits, most Brittanys remain healthy and active for more than a decade. Your older Brittany may not run as fast or hear as well as when he was younger, but he needs your love and attention as much as ever.

Resources

Associations and Organizations

Breed Clubs

American Brittany Club
clubs.akc.org/brit/

American Kennel Club (AKC)
5580 Centerview Drive
Raleigh, NC 27606
Telephone: (919) 233-9767
Fax: (919) 233-3627
E-Mail: info@akc.org
www.akc.org

Canadian Kennel Club (CKC)
89 Skyway Avenue, Suite 100
Etobicoke, Ontario M9W 6R4
Telephone: (416) 675-5511
Fax: (416) 675-6506
E-Mail: information@ckc.ca
www.ckc.ca

Federation Cynologique Internationale (FCI)
Secretariat General de la FCI
Place Albert 1er, 13
B – 6530 Thuin
Belqique
www.fci.be

The Brittany Club of Great Britain
www.brittanyclub.co.uk

The Kennel Club
1 Clarges Street
London
W1J 8AB
Telephone: 0870 606 6750
Fax: 0207 518 1058
www.the-kennel-club.org.uk

United Kennel Club (UKC)
100 E. Kilgore Road
Kalamazoo, MI 49002-5584
Telephone: (269) 343-9020
Fax: (269) 343-7037
E-Mail: pbickell@ukcdogs.com
www.ukcdogs.com

Pet Sitters

National Association of Professional Pet Sitters
15000 Commerce Parkway, Suite C
Mt. Laurel, New Jersey 08054
Telephone: (856) 439-0324
Fax: (856) 439-0525
E-Mail: napps@ahint.com
www.petsitters.org

Pet Sitters International
201 East King Street
King, NC 27021-9161
Telephone: (336) 983-9222
Fax: (336) 983-5266
E-Mail: info@petsit.com
www.petsit.com

Rescue Organizations and Animal Welfare Groups

American Brittany Rescue
Secretary
63 Grove St, Oakland, NJ 07436
www.americanbrittanyrescue.org

American Humane Association (AHA)
63 Inverness Drive East
Englewood, CO 80112
Telephone: (303) 792-9900
Fax: 792-5333
www.americanhumane.org

American Society for the Prevention of Cruelty to Animals (ASPCA)
424 E. 92nd Street
New York, NY 10128-6804
Telephone: (212) 876-7700
www.aspca.org

Royal Society for the Prevention of Cruelty to Animals (RSPCA)
RSPCA Enquiries Service
Wilberforce Way, Southwater,
Horsham, West Sussex RH13 9RS
United Kingdom
Telephone: 0870 3335 999
Fax: 0870 7530 284
www.rspca.org.uk

Sports
International Agility Link (IAL)
Global Administrator: Steve Drinkwater
E-Mail: yunde@powerup.au
www.agilityclick.com/~ial

The World Canine Freestyle Organization, Inc.
P.O. Box 350122
Brooklyn, NY 11235
Telephone: (718) 332-8336
Fax: (718) 646-2686
E-Mail: WCFODOGS@aol.com
www.worldcaninefreestyle.org

Therapy
Delta Society
875 124th Ave, NE, Suite 101
Bellevue, WA 98005
Telephone: (425) 679-5500
Fax: (425) 679-5539
E-Mail: info@DeltaSociety.org
www.deltasociety.org

Therapy Dogs Inc.
P.O. Box 20227
Cheyenne WY 82003
Telephone: (877) 843-7364
Fax: (307) 638-2079
E-Mail: therapydogsinc@qwestoffice.net
www.therapydogs.com

Therapy Dogs International (TDI)
88 Bartley Road
Flanders, NJ 07836
Telephone: (973) 252-9800
Fax: (973) 252-7171
E-Mail: tdi@gti.net
www.tdi-dog.org

Training
Association of Pet Dog Trainers (APDT)
150 Executive Center Drive Box 35
Greenville, SC 29615
Telephone: (800) PET-DOGS
Fax: (864) 331-0767
E-Mail: information@apdt.com
www.apdt.com

International Association of Animal Behavior Consultants (IAABC)
565 Callery Road
Cranberry Township, PA 16066
E-Mail: info@iaabc.org
www.iaabc.org

National Association of Dog Obedience Instructors (NADOI)
PMB 369
729 Grapevine Hwy.
Hurst, TX 76054-2085
www.nadoi.org

Veterinary and Health Resources

Academy of Veterinary Homeopathy (AVH)
P.O. Box 9280
Wilmington, DE 19809
Telephone: (866) 652-1590
Fax: (866) 652-1590
www.theavh.org

American Academy of Veterinary Acupuncture (AAVA)
P.O. Box 1058
Glastonbury, CT 06033
Telephone: (860) 632-9911
Fax: (860) 659-8772
www.aava.org

American Animal Hospital Association (AAHA)
12575 W. Bayaud Ave.
Lakewood, CO 80228
Telephone: (303) 986-2800
Fax: (303) 986-1700
E-Mail: info@aahanet.org
www.aahanet.org/index.cfm

American College of Veterinary Internal Medicine (ACVIM)
1997 Wadsworth Blvd., Suite A
Lakewood, CO 80214-5293
Telephone: (800) 245-9081
Fax: (303) 231-0880
Email: ACVIM@ACVIM.org
www.acvim.org

American College of Veterinary Ophthalmologists (ACVO)
P.O. Box 1311
Meridian, ID 83860
Telephone: (208) 466-7624
Fax: (208) 466-7693
E-Mail: office09@acvo.com
www.acvo.com

American Holistic Veterinary Medical Association (AHVMA)
2218 Old Emmorton Road
Bel Air, MD 21015
Telephone: (410) 569-0795
Fax: (410) 569-2346
E-Mail: office@ahvma.org
www.ahvma.org

American Veterinary Medical Association (AVMA)
1931 North Meacham Road, Suite 100
Schaumburg, IL 60173-4360
Telephone: (847) 925-8070
Fax: (847) 925-1329
E-Mail: avmainfo@avma.org
www.avma.org

ASPCA Animal Poison Control Center
Telephone: (888) 426-4435
www.aspca.org

British Veterinary Association (BVA)
7 Mansfield Street
London
W1G 9NQ
Telephone: 0207 636 6541
Fax: 0207 908 6349
E-Mail: bvahq@bva.co.uk
www.bva.co.uk

Canine Eye Registration Foundation (CERF)
VMDB/CERF
1717 Philo Rd
P O Box 3007
Urbana, IL 61803-3007
Telephone: (217) 693-4800
Fax: (217) 693-4801
E-Mail: CERF@vmbd.org
www.vmdb.org

Orthopedic Foundation for Animals (OFA)
2300 NE Nifong Blvd
Columbus, Missouri 65201-3856
Telephone: (573) 442-0418
Fax: (573) 875-5073
Email: ofa@offa.org
www.offa.org

US Food and Drug Administration Center for Veterinary Medicine (CVM)
7519 Standish Place
HFV-12
Rockville, MD 20855-0001
Telephone: (240) 276-9300 or (888) INFO-FDA
http://www.fda.gov/cvm

Publications

Books

Anderson, Teoti. *The Super Simple Guide to Housetraining.* Neptune City: TFH Publications, 2004.

Anne, Jonna, with Mary Straus. *The Healthy Dog Cookbook: 50 Nutritious and Delicious Recipes Your Dog Will Love.* UK: Ivy Press Limited, 2008.

Boneham, Sheila Webster. *Training Your Dog for Life.* TFH, 2008.

Boneham, Sheila Webster. *Rescue Matters! How to Find, Foster, and Rehome Companion Animals.* Alpine Publications, 2009.

Dainty, Suellen. *50 Games to Play With Your Dog.* UK: Ivy Press Limited, 2007.

Morgan, Diane. *Good Dogkeeping.* Neptune City: TFH Publications, 2005.

Magazines

AKC Family Dog
American Kennel Club
260 Madison Avenue
New York, NY 10016
Telephone: (800) 490-5675
E-Mail: familydog@akc.org
www.akc.org/pubs/familydog

AKC Gazette
American Kennel Club
260 Madison Avenue
New York, NY 10016
Telephone: (800) 533-7323
E-Mail: gazette@akc.org
www.akc.org/pubs/gazette

Dog & Kennel
Pet Publishing, Inc.
7-L Dundas Circle
Greensboro, NC 27407
Telephone: (336) 292-4272
Fax: (336) 292-4272
E-Mail: info@petpublishing.com
www.dogandkennel.com

Dogs Monthly
Ascot House
High Street, Ascot,
Berkshire SL5 7JG
United Kingdom
Telephone: 0870 730 8433
Fax: 0870 730 8431
E-Mail: admin@rtc-associates.freeserve.co.uk
www.corsini.co.uk/dogsmonthly

Websites

Nylabone
www.nylabone.com

Rescue Matters
www.rescuematters.com

TFH Publications, Inc.
www.tfh.com

Index

Note: **Boldfaced** numbers indicate illustrations.

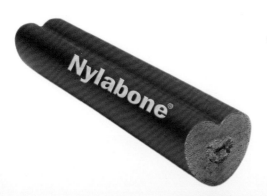

Photo Credits

Dedication

For Lily and Jay, who get me away from the computer when I lose track of time. Good dogs!

Acknowledgments

Many thanks to the dedicated fans of the Brittany, to the owners, breeders, and rescuers too nuerous to name who shared their thoughts and knowledge with me, and to the beautiful Brittanys I've met and admired through the years.

About the Author

Sheila Webster Boneham, Ph.D., loves animals and writing about animals. Three of her books have won the prestigious Maxwell Award from the Dog Writers Asociation of America. Sheila lives in Nevada with her husband Roger and their canine companions, and has long been active in canine sports, rescue, breeding, therapy work, and good hairy fun. In addition to writing, Sheila teaches workshops on pet rescue and on writing; you can contact her through her website at http://www.sheilaboneham.com.

Nylabone®

He **Plays** Hard.
He **Chews** Hard.

He's a **Nylabone**® Dog!

Your #1 choice for healthy chews & treats.

Nylabone proudly offers high-quality durable chews,
delicious edible treats, and fun, interactive toys for dogs of all sizes, shapes, and life stages.

Nylabone Products • P.O. Box 427, Neptune, NJ 07754-0427 • 1-800-631-2188 • Fax: 732-988-5466
www.nylabone.com • info@nylabone.com • For more information contact your sales representative or contact us at sales@tfh.com

A318